East India Company

Authentic Papers Concerning India Affairs

Which have Been under the Inspection of a Great Assembly

East India Company

Authentic Papers Concerning India Affairs
Which have Been under the Inspection of a Great Assembly

ISBN/EAN: 9783337139575

Printed in Europe, USA, Canada, Australia, Japan

Cover: Foto ©ninafisch / pixelio.de

More available books at **www.hansebooks.com**

AUTHENTIC PAPERS

CONCERNING

INDIA AFFAIRS;

WHICH HAVE BEEN UNDER THE INSPECTION

OF A

GREAT ASSEMBLY.

LONDON:
Printed for RICHARDSON and URQUHART, under the Royal Exchange.
MDCCLXXI.

TO THE
READER.

THE following publications are of transcripts, faithfully made from authentic copies of original letters; free, it is hoped, of all but such trivial errors as are incident to transcriptions, or unavoidable from the press.

They contain representations of weighty matters, made by rival parties, while contending for power in India; and, therefore, may respectively be considered, abstractedly from all the direct information which they furnish, as useful comments on each other: so that they will serve, in no inconsiderable degree, to ascertain the comparative talents, principles, practices and views of violent antagonists, in their discharge of such public trusts as were highly interesting to all men, while they demonstrate the nature of our territorial connections with Hindostan, which are now of such infinite importance to the Company and the State: and they, moreover, inform us of the regulations that were made for the preservation of those possessions.

Time, the only true test of all human policy, has now enabled us, with some certainty, to decide on the wisdom and rectitude of measures that were then planned and pursued, from the effects they have produced; which perhaps may be best ascertained, by examining and estimating the present state of the Company's affairs and finances, both in England and India; the condition of the native Asiatics, and likewise of the generality of British subjects in Bengal; as also the extraordinary effects of much-boasted reformations; how far confident prophesies have really been fulfilled, of approaching high prosperity to the Company,

pany, and of proportionable welfare to all in their employ; with obferving who have fooneft and moft enriched themfelves by tranfactions in the Eaft.

Thefe letters will befides furnifh us with fome, though but a very faint idea of what, for feveral years paft, the ftate of juftice has been in India: and likewife difcover in how arbitrary and unconftitutional a manner mere power has been made to operate in thofe regions, efpecially with regard to the natives, who are defencelefs, and not unfrequently, through them, even on the fubjects of this kingdom. Thofe related in thefe letters were, however, but leading tranfactions of outrage to infinitely worfe, that very fpeedily followed, from the moft wanton indulgences in rapine and defpotifm; of which the public may expect to acquire knowledge from farther publications. But to prevent the ruinous effects in future of power fo exercifed, it fhould be hoped legiflative government will
very

very strongly interpose; as well for the due encouragement of merit, by affording it protection, as for the honour of our national justice, the advancement of the general interest, and for the effectual preservation of extensive, populous and wealthy provinces, which can be no other than the property of the State.

Let it not, however, be mistakenly apprehended, that there is any intention whatever, by making this publication, to favour any party or individual, or to extenuate any kind of real guilt or misconduct. The sole end in view being, by exhibited facts and proofs, to shew what the nature of our India connexions really is; to demonstrate what policy and practice have been with regard to them; to shew what kinds of power and justice are prevalent in those countries, and to set wise men upon considering what effects they have already produced, what farther they naturally may be expected to produce, d...e, or what a yet more weak or evil conduct may unhappily effect; to the prejudice of the subjected natives, of individual Europeans, the East-India Company, and this nation in general.

CONTENTS,

CONTENTS.

I.

COPY of a LETTER from the Right Hon. Lord CLIVE, to the COURT of DIRECTORS of the EAST-INDIA COMPANY   Page 1

II.

COPY of a LETTER from the Right Hon. Lord CLIVE, and the reſt of the SELECT COMMITTEE, at Fort William in BENGAL, to the COURT of DIRECTORS of the EAST-INDIA COMPANY   55

III.

COPY of a LETTER from Meſſ. RALPH LEYCESTER and GEORGE GRAY, Members of the Council at FORT WILLIAM; addreſſed to the COURT of DIrectors of the EAST-INDIA COMPANY   107

COPY

COPY OF A LETTER

FROM

THE RIGHT HON. LORD CLIVE,

TO THE

COURT OF DIRECTORS

OF THE EAST-INDIA-COMPANY.

CALCUTTA, 30th September 1765.

GENTLEMEN,

1st. BY the letter from the Select Committee, and copy of their proceedings, which are transmitted to you by this conveyance, you will be enabled to form a general idea of the state of this settlement on the arrival of the ship Kent; together with the measures we thought necessary to pursue, in order to settle the Company's

A

pany's affairs in these provinces upon an advantageous and permanent foundation. You will permit me, however, to lay before you my own sentiments in particular concerning those measures, and to communicate also, by this earliest opportunity, such others as I wish should be adopted before I quit the government: and which I hope will be not only approved of, but likewise so fully confirmed and established by the Court of Directors, that the abuses which may otherwise be revived by the ambition and avarice of some future Governors, or Councils, may be effectually prevented.

2d. Upon my arrival, I am sorry to say, I found your affairs in a condition so nearly desperate, as would have alarmed any set of men, whose sense of honour and duty to their employers had not been estranged by the too eager pursuit of their own immediate advantages. The sudden, and, among many, the unwarrantable acquisition of riches had introduced luxury in every shape, and in its most pernicious excess. These two enormous evils went hand in hand together through the whole presidency, infecting
almost

almost every member of each department: every inferior seemed to have grasped at wealth, that he might be enabled to assume that spirit of profusion which was now the only distinction between him and his superior. Thus all distinction ceased, and every rank became in a manner upon an equality: nor was this the end of the mischief; for a contest of such a nature, among your servants, necessarily destroyed all proportion between their wants and the honest means of satisfying them. /In a country where money is plenty, where fear is the principle of government, where your arms are ever victorious; in such a country, I say, it is no wonder that corruption should find its way to a spot so well prepared to receive it: it is no wonder, that the lust of riches should readily embrace the proffered means of its gratification, or that the instruments of your power should avail themselves of their authority, and proceed even to extortion in those cases where simple corruption could not keep pace with their rapacity/ Examples of this sort, set by superiors, could not fail of being followed in a proportionable degree by inferiors. The evil

evil was contagious, and spread among both civil and military, down to the writer, the enſign and the free merchant.

3d. The large ſums of money acquired by donation, beſides the means I have already mentioned, were ſo publicly known and vindicated, that every one thought he had a right to enrich himſelf at all events, with as much expedition as poſſible. The monopoly of ſalt, beetel, tobacco, &c. was another fund of immenſe profits to the Company's ſervants, and likewiſe to ſuch others as they permitted to enjoy a ſhare; while not a rupee of advantage accrued to the Government, and very little to the Company from that trade. Before I had diſcovered theſe various ſources of wealth, I was under great aſtoniſhment to find individuals ſo ſuddenly enriched, that there was ſcarce a gentleman in the ſettlement who had not fixed upon a very ſhort period for his return to England with affluence. From hence aroſe that froward ſpirit of independency which in a manner ſet all your orders at defiance, and dictated a total contempt

tempt of them, as often as obedience was found incompatible with private intereſt. At the time of my arrival, I ſaw nothing that bore the form, or appearance of government. The authority and pre-eminence of the Governor were levelled with thoſe of the Councillors; every Councillor was as much a Governor, as he who bore the name; and diſtinction of rank, as I have already obſerved, was no longer to be found in the whole ſettlement. Notwithſtanding a ſpecial order from the Court of Directors, founded on very wiſe and very evident reaſons, that all correſpondence with the country powers ſhould be carried on ſolely in the Governor's name, I found that our whole correſpondence with the Great Mogul, the Subahs, Nabobs and Rajas had been of late carried on by, and in the name of the whole Board; and that every ſervant and free merchant correſponded with whom they pleaſed.

4th. Your orders for the execution of the covenants were poſitive, and expreſly mentioned to be the reſolution of a General Court of Proprietors. Your ſervants at at Bengal, however, abſolutely determined to rejeƈt them: and had not the Seleƈt Committee reſolved, that the example ſhould be firſt ſet by the Council, or a ſuſpenſion from your ſervice take place, it is certain they would have remained unexecuted to this hour. You will not, I imagine, be much ſurprized at this breach of duty, if you look over the general letter; where you cannot avoid ſeeing how many are annually committed, and how faſt every thing was tending to a contempt of your authority. From a ſhort ſurvey of the late tranſactions I was convinced, that no other remedy was left than an immediate and vigorous exertion of the powers with which the Committee weie inveſted. Happy, in my opinion, was it for the Company, that ſuch powers were granted, for that the ſettlement, ſo conduƈted, could have ſubſiſted another twelvemonth appears to me an impoſſibility. A great part of the revenues of the country, amounting to near four millions ſterling *per annum*, would have been divided among your ſervants: and the acquiſition of fortunes being ſo ſudden, a few months muſt

muſt have brought writers into council: ſeniority muſt have been admitted as a juſt claim to a ſeat at the Board, without the qualification of age or experience, becauſe the rapidity of ſucceſſion denied the attainment of either.

5th. Nor were theſe exceſſes confined to your civil ſervants alone: the military department alſo had caught the infection, and riches, the bane of diſcipline, were daily promoting the ruin of your army. The too little inequality of rank rendered the advantages of Captains, Lieutenants and Enſigns ſo nearly upon a par, and ſo large, that an independent fortune was no diſtant proſpect even to a ſubaltern. If a too quick ſucceſſion among thoſe from whom you expect the ſtudy of commerce and polity is detrimental to your civil concerns, how effectually deſtructive that evil muſt prove to your military operations. The moſt experienced European officer, when he has entered into the Eaſt India ſervice, although he may be able in many points to ſuggeſt improvements to others, will neverthelefs find that ſomething new remains for himſelf to learn peculiar to this ſervice,

which

which cannot be attained in a day. Judge then how the case must stand with youths, who are either just sent out from the academy, or, which more frequently happens, who have had no education at all; for to such have we often been reduced to the necessity of granting commissions. How much must the expectation of your army be raised when they are suffered, without controul, to take possession for themselves of the whole booty, donation-money and plunder, on the capture of a city? This I can assure you happened at Benares; and what is more surprizing, the then Governor and Council, so far from laying in a claim to the moiety, which ought to have been reserved for the Company, agreeable to those positive orders from the Court of Directors a few years ago, when they were pleased to put their forces upon the same footing as those of his Majesty, gave up the whole to the captors. You have hear'd of the general mutiny that happened among your Seapoys a little before my arrival. What would have been your consternation, had you also hear'd of an unanimous desertion of your European

European soldiery? These were very serious events indeed: and had it not been for one well-timed, vigorous act of Major Munro, and the unwearied zeal and military abilities of General Carnac, who totally suppressed the spirit of mutiny among the soldiers, your possessions in India might at this time have been destitute of a man to support them, and even the privilege of commerce irrecoverably crushed.] Common justice to the principles and conduct of General Carnac obliges me farther to add, that I found him the only officer of rank who had resisted the temptations, to which by his station he was constantly subject, of acquiring an immense fortune: and I question much whether he is not the only man who has of late years been honoured with the command of your forces, without acquiring a very large independency. The letter from the Great Mogul to the Governor and Council, requesting their permission for him to accept a present of two laak, which his Majesty is desirous of bestowing on him, as a reward for his disinterested services, will corroborate what I have said in his favour: and as

B this

this affair, agreeable to the tenor of the covenants, is referred to the Court of Directors, I make no doubt they will readily embrace the opportunity of shewing their regard to such diftinguished merit, by confenting to his acceptance of his Majefty's bounty.

6th. If the picture I have drawn be a faithful likenefs of this prefidency; and I call upon the moft guilty, for guilty there are, to shew that I have aggravated a feature; to what a deplorable condition muft your affairs have foon been reduced? Every ftate (and fuch now is your government in India) muft be near its period, when the rage of luxury and corruption has feized upon its leaders and inhabitants. Can trade be encouraged for public benefit, where the management unfortunately devolves upon thofe who make private intereft their rule of action? And farther, has fudden affluence ever failed, from the infancy of difcipline to the prefent perfection of it, to corrupt the principle and deftroy the fpirit of an army? Independency of fortune is always averfe to thofe duties of fubordination which are infeparable from the

life

life of a soldier: and in this country, if the acquisition be sudden, a relaxation of discipline is more immediately the consequence. I would not be thought, by these observations, to exclude riches from the military. Honour alone is scarcely a sufficient reward for the toilsome service of the field. But the acquisition of wealth ought to be so gradual as to admit not a prospect of compleating it, till succession by merit to the rank of a field officer should have laid a good foundation for the claim. Such is the idea I entertained of this matter when I delivered my sentiments to the Court of Directors, in my letter of the 27th April 1764; and I have acted in conformity thereto by regimenting the troops in the manner I then proposed. I need not repeat the observations I troubled you with in that letter: it is sufficient to remark here, that the good effects of the plan are already visible; that subordination is restored, abuses corrected, and your expences, of course, already greatly diminished.

7th. The war which, to my great concern, I found extended above 700 miles from

from the prefidency, is now happily concluded; and a peace eftablifhed upon terms which promife lafting tranquillity to thefe provinces. This event has, I find, difappointed the expectations of many, who thought of nothing but a march with the King to Delhi.

My refolution however was, and my hope will always be, to confine our affiftance, our conquefts, and our poffeffions to Bengal, Bahar, and Orixa. To go farther is, in my opinion, a fcheme fo extravagantly ambitious and abfurd, that no Governor and Council, in their fenfes, can ever adopt it, unlefs the whole fyftem of the Company's intereft be firft intirely new modelled.

8th. I forbear troubling you with a detail of the negociations of General Carnac, and me with the country powers, and the particulars of the treaty of peace with the Vifier of the empire, as they will be fpoken of at large in the letter from the Select Committee, and appear likewife upon the face of our proceedings. I will, however, juft remark, that our reftoring to Shuga Dowla the whole of his dominions, proceeds more from the

policy

policy of not extending the Company's territorial poffeffions than the generous principle of attaching him for ever to our intereft by gratitude, though this has been the apparent, and is by many thought to be the real motive. Had we ambitioufly attempted to retain the conquered country, experience would foon have proved the abfurdity and impracticability of fuch a plan. The eftablifhment of your army muft have been largely increafed, a confiderable number of civil fervants muft have been added to your lift, and more chiefships appointed. The acts of oppreffion and innumerable abufes which would have been committed, and which could neither have been prevented nor remedied at fo great a diftance from the prefidency, muft infallibly have laid the foundation of another war, deftructive and unfuccefsful: our old privileges and poffeffions would have been endangered by every fupply we might have been tempted to afford in fupport of the new, and the natives muft have finally triumphed in our inability to fuftain the weight of our own ambition.

9th.

9th. To return to the point from which this digreſſion has led me, I muſt carry you back to the deſcription, above given, of the ſituation in which I found your affairs on my arrival. Two paths were evidently open to me: the one ſmooth, and ſtrewed with abundance of rich advantages that might eaſily be picked up; the other untrodden, and every ſtep oppoſed with obſtacles. I might have taken charge of the government upon the ſame footing on which I found it; that is, I might have enjoyed the name of Governor, and have ſuffered the honour, importance, and dignity of the poſt to continue in their ſtate of annihilation. I might have contented myſelf, as others had before me, with being a cypher, or what is little better, the firſt among ſixteen equals; and I might have been allowed this paſſive conduct to be attended with the uſual douceur of ſharing largely with the reſt of the gentlemen in all donations, perquiſites, &c. ariſing from the abſolute government and diſpoſal of all places in the revenues of this opulent kingdom; by which means I might ſoon have acquired an immenſe addition to my fortune,

tune, notwithstanding the obligations in the new covenants; for the man who can so easily get over the bar of conscience, as to receive presents after the execution of them, will not scruple to make use of any evasions that may protect him from the consequences. The settlement in general would thus have been my friends, and only the natives of the country my enemies. If you can conceive a Governor in such a situation, it is impossible to form a wrong judgment of the inferior servants, or of the Company's affairs at such a presidency. An honourable alternative, however, lay before me. I had the power, within my own breast, to fullfill the duty of my station, by remaining incorruptible in the midst of numberless temptations artfully thrown in my way, by exposing my character to every attack which malice or resentment are so apt to invent against any man who attempts reformation, and by encountering, of course, the odium of the settlement. I hesitated not a moment which choice to make. I took upon my shoulders a burden which required resolution, perseverance, and constitution to support. Having chosen

my

my part I was determined to exert myself in the attempt; happy in the reflection, that the honour of the nation and the very being of the company would be maintained by the fuccefs; and confcious that, if I failed, my integrity and good intentions at leaft muft remain unimpeached. The other members of the committee joined with me in opinion, that in order to proceed upon bufinefs it was abfolutely neceffary for us to affume the powers wherewith we were invefted. We faw plainly, that moft of the gentlemen in council had been too deeply concerned themfelves, in the meafures which required amendment, for us to expect any affiftance from them; on the contrary, we were certain of finding oppofition to every plan of innovation, and an unanimous attempt to defeat the intentions of the proprietors, who folicited my acceptance of the government. The Committee, therefore, immediately met, and I had the happinefs to find myfelf fupported by gentlemen whom no temptations could feduce, no inconveniencies, or threats of malice deter. Our proceedings will convince you, that we have

dared,

dared to act with firmness and integrity, and will at the same time demonstrate, that temper, unanimity, and dispatch must ever mark the proceedings of men unbiassed by private interest.

10th. The gentlemen in council of late years at Bengal seem to have been actuated, in every consultation, by a very obstinate and mischievous spirit. The office of Governor has been in a manner hunted down, stripped of its dignity, and then divided into sixteen shares. Whether ambition, obstinacy, pride, or self-interest is usually the motive to such a pursuit, I will not take upon me to determine; but am sure it can never arise from a just idea of government, or a true sense of the Company's interest. In my opinion, it is the duty of the Council to make the power of the president appear as extensive as possible in the eyes of the people, that all correspondence with the country princes should be carried on through him alone, some particular cases excepted; that the Council should upon all occasions be unanimous in supporting, not in extenuating the dignity of his station; and that he ought to be considered

sidered among the natives as the sole manager and conductor of political affairs. This should be the outward appearance of administration: though in reality, the Council must be allowed a freedom of judgment; and when they perceive in the Governor a tendency to absolute, or unjustifiable measures, it then becomes their duty to check him. If they at any time have reason to distrust the rectitude of his principles, they should not allow him to execute designs, even of the smallest moment, without previously laying them before the Board, and obtaining their approbation. In short, the best Governor should not, except in cases of necessity, be suffered to conclude any points of importance without the sanction of the Board. But the expedient of a Select Committee equally prevents any ill conduct in the Governor, and is besides attended with advantages which can rarely be expected from the whole body of Councillors. Five gentlemen well versed in the Company's true interest, of abilities to plan, and resolution to execute; gentlemen whose fortunes are honourably approaching to affluence, and whose

integrity

integrity has never suffered them to exceed the bounds of moderation: a Select Committee composed of such men will transact more business in a week than the Council can in a month. The opinions and judgment of five men are as securely to be relied on, even in affairs of the utmost consequence, as sixteen; they are less liable to dissension, and it may be said, beyond a contradiction, that their administration is more distant from democratic anarchy. The Council would not be, however, an useless body: for whilst the attention of the Committee was chiefly engaged in watching and repairing the main springs of government, the Council would as materially serve the Company in attending to the many other movements of the grand machine, which are as essentially necessary to the public advantage and security; and that the Committee should not be able to carry their powers to any dangerous length, they might be ordered annually, before the dispatch of the Europe ships, to submit their proceedings to the review of the gentlemen in council, who might transmit their opinions thereupon to the Court of Directors. Your present Select Committee have, from time to time, laid most of their proceedings before Council; and we intend to continue the same system of candor, except in any political cases of secrecy, when prudence may require that our resolutions should be confined to the knowledge of a few.

11th. Thus freely I have given you my opinion upon the sort of government I could wish to see established in this settlement; nor shall I think my duty done till I have pointed out every measure that seems to me best calculated to preserve your affairs from destruction. At Bengal, the rule of succession among your servants is perniciously exact: there are frequent occasions where it ought to be set aside: where experience, understanding, integrity, moderation ought to take place of accidental seniority. The demerits of most of your superior servants have been so great, as you learn from the Committee proceedings, that one can hardly imagine their future behaviour will entitle them to farther favours than you have hitherto bestowed on them. I do not pretend to surmise what sentence you may

may pronounce upon the gentlemen who came under the cenfure of the Committee, but whether it be moderate as ours, or fevere as it deferves, it will not much concern them, fince all of them are now in very affluent circumftances, and will probably return to Europe by this or the next year's fhipping. Perufe then the lift of your covenanted fervants upon this eftablifhment. You will find that many of thofe next in fucceffion are not only very young in the fervice, and confefequently unfit for fuch exalted ftations, but are alfo ftrongly tainted with the principles of their fuperiors. If your opinion fhould correfpond with mine, fome remedy will be judged neceffary to be applied; and I confefs I fee but one. The unhappy change which within thefe few years has arifen in the manners and conduct of your fervants at Bengal, is alone fufficient to remove the objections I once had to appointments from another fettlement: and the difficulty which now too plainly appears of filling up vacancies in Council with the requifite attention to the Company's honour and welfare, inclines me to wifh fuch appointments more frequent.

frequent. In the prefent ftate of this prefidency, no meafure can, I think, prove more falutary than to appoint five or fix gentlemen from the Coaft to the Bengal eftablifhment, and there to poft them agreeable to their rank and ftanding in the fervice. Meff. Ruffell, Floyer, Alderfey, and Kelfall are among thofe who would be very well worthy your attention, if this plan fhould be adopted. I cannot help farther recommending to your confideration, whether, if every other method fhould be found ineffectual, the tranfplanting a few of the young Bengal fervants to Madrafs would not be of fignal fervice, both to themfelves and the Company. You will likewife confider whether the fettlement of Bombay is capable of furnifhing us with a few meritorious fervants. With regard to Madrafs, the conduct of the gentlemen upon that eftablifhment is in general fo unexceptionable, that to prefent Bengal with fuch examples of regularity, difcretion, and moderation would, I think, be a means of reftoring it to good order and government. It is paft a doubt, that every attempt of reformation muft fail,

unlefs

unless the superior servants be exemplary in their principles and conduct. If we see nothing but rapacity among Councillors, in vain shall we look for moderation among writers.

12th. The sources of tyranny and oppression which have been opened by European Agents, acting under the authority of the Company's Servants, and the numberless black Agents and Sub-agents acting also under them, will, I fear, be a lasting reproach to the English name in this country. It is impossible to enumerate the complaints that have been laid before me by the unfortunate inhabitants, who had not forgot that I was an enemy to oppression. The necessity of securing the confidence of the natives is an idea I have ever maintained, and was in hopes would be invariably adopted by others: but ambition, success, and luxury have, I find, introduced a new system of politics, at the severe expence of English honour, of the Company's faith, and even of common justice and humanity. The orders so frequently issued, that no writer shall have the privilege of dustucks, I have strictly obeyed: but I am sorry

to

to inform you that all the wished-for consequences are not to be expected. The officers of the Government are so sensible of our influence and authority, that they dare not presume to search or stop a boat protected by the name of a Company's servant; and you may be assured, that frauds of that kind, so easy to be practised and so difficult to be detected, are but too frequent. I have at last, however, the happiness to see the completion of an event which in this respect, as well as in many others, must be productive of advantages hitherto unknown; and at the same time prevent abuses that have hitherto had no remedy. I mean the Dewannee, which is the superintendancy of all the lands and the collection of all the revenues of the provinces of Bengal, Bahar, and Orixa. The assistance which the Great Mogul had received from our arms and treasury, made him readily bestow this grant upon the Company: and it is done in the most effectual manner you can desire. The allowance for the support of the Nabob's dignity and power, and the tribute to his Majesty, must be regularly paid; the remainder belongs to to the Company. Revolutions are now no longer to be apprehended; the means of affecting them will in future be wanting to ambitious Muſſulmen: nor will your ſervants, civil or military, be tempted to foment diſturbances, from whence can ariſe no benefit to themſelves. Reſtitution, donation-money, &c. &c. will be perfectly aboliſhed, as the revenues from whence they uſed to iſſue will be poſſeſſed by ourſelves. The power of ſuperviſing the provinces, though lodged in us, ſhould not however, in my opinion, be exerted. Three times the preſent number of civil ſervants would be inſufficient for the purpoſe: whereas, if we leave the management to the old officers of the government, the Company need not be at the expence of one additional ſervant; and though we may ſuffer in the collection, yet we ſhall always be able to detect and puniſh any great offenders, and ſhall have ſome ſatisfaction in knowing that the corruption is not among ourſelves. By this means alſo the abuſes inevitably ſpringing from the exerciſe of territorial authority will be effectually obviated: there will still be a Nabob, with an allowance suitable to his dignity; and the territorial jurisdiction will still be in the chiefs of the country, acting under him and the presidency in conjunction, though the revenues will belong to the Company. Besides, were the Company's officers to be the collectors, foreign nations would immediately take umbrage; and complaints preferred to the British Court might be attended with very embarrassing consequences. Nor can it be supposed that either the French, Dutch, or Danes will acknowledge the English Company Nabob of Bengal, and pay into the hands of their servants the duties upon trade, or the quit-rents of those districts which they have for many years possessed, by virtue of the Royal Phirmaund, or by grants from former Nabobs.

13th. Your revenues, by means of this new acquisition, will, as near as I can judge, not fall short, for the ensuing year, of 250 laaks of Sicca rupees, including your former possessions of Burdwan, &c. Hereafter they will at least amount to 20 or 30 laaks more. Your civil and military expences in time of peace can

can never exceed 60 laaks of rupees. The Nabobs allowances are already reduced to 42 laaks, and the tribute to the King is fixed at 26. So that there will be remaining a clear gain to the Company of 122 laaks of Sicca rupees, or 1,650,900 l. sterling: which will defray all the expences of the inveftments, furnish the whole of the China treafure, anfwer the demands of all your other fettlements in India, and leave a confiderable balance in your treafury befides. In time of war, when the country may be fubject to the incurfions of bodies of cavalry, we fhall, notwithftanding, be able to collect a fufficient fum for our civil and military exigencies, and likewife for our inveftments; becaufe a very rich part of the Bengal and Bahar dominions are fituated to the eaftward of the Ganges, where we can never be invaded. What I have given you is a real, not an imaginary ftate of your revenues; and you may be affured they will not fall fhort of my computation.

14th. Permit me here to have the honour of laying before you one ftriking circumftance, which has occurred to me in considering the subject of the Dewannee, and the consequences of your large increase of revenues. I have already observed, that our acquisition will give no umbrage to foreign nations, with respect to our territorial jurisdiction, so long as the present appearance of the Nabob's power is preserved; but I am convinced they will e'er long entertain jealousies of our commercial superiority. Public complaints have indeed been already made from both French and Dutch factories, that the dread of the English name, added to the encouragement of your servants at the different Aurungs, has *deterred* the weavers from complying with their usual and necessary demands: and I am persuaded that, sooner or later, national remonstrances will be made on that subject. Perhaps one half of the trade being reserved to the English Company, and the other divided between the French, Dutch and Danes, in such proportions as may be settled between their respective Commissaries, might adjust these disputes to the mutual satisfaction of all parties. Besides, as every nation which trades to the East-Indies constantly

brings

brings out silver, for the purchase of merchandize in return, and as our revenues will for the future enable us to furnish all our investments without any remittance from England, it seems necessary that we should, in some degree, encourage the trade of others, in order that this country may be supplied by them with Bullion, to replace the quantity we shall annually send to China, or to any other part of the world. It is impossible for me to be a sufficient judge of the practicability, or propriety of admitting other nations to such a proportion of trade with us in these parts, nor will you suspect that I entertain a thought of taking any step without instructions from you in an affair of such national importance. I do not even presume to argue upon the subject: I only mention it as a point which has occurred to me, and which I think well merits your most serious consideration.

15th. Considering the excesses we have of late years manifested in our conduct, the princes of Indostan will not readily imagine us capable of moderation; nor can we expect they will ever be attached

tached to us by any other motive than fear. Meer Jaffier Coffim Ally, the prefent Nabob, and even Mahomed Ally, the Nabob of Arcot (the beft Muffulman I ever knew) have afforded inftances fufficient of their inclinations to throw off the Englifh fuperiority. No opportunity will ever be neglected that feems to favor an attempt to extirpate us, though the confequences, while we keep our army complete, muft in the end be more fatal to themfelves. This impatience under the fubjection, as I may call it, to Europeans is natural: but fo great is the infatuation of the natives of this country, that they look no farther than the prefent moment, and will put their all to the hazard of a fingle battle. Even our young Nabob, who is the iffue of a proftitute, who has little abilities, and lefs education to fupply the want of them; mean, weak, and ignorant as this man is, he would, if left to himfelf and a few of his artful flatterers, purfue the very paths of his predeceffors. It is impoffible, therefore, to truft him with power and be fafe. If you mean to maintain your prefent poffeffions and advantages,

tages, the command of the army and receipt of the revenues muſt be kept in your own hands. Every wiſh he may expreſs to obtain either, be aſſured, is an indication of his deſire to reduce you to your original ſtate of dependency, to which you can never now return without ceaſing to exiſt. If you allow the Nabob to have forces, he will ſoon raiſe money: if you allow him a full treaſury, without forces, he will certainly make uſe of it to invite the Marattas, or other powers, to invade the country, upon a ſuppoſition that we ſhall not ſuſpect the part he takes, and that ſucceſs will reſtore him to the full extent of his ſovereignty; for ſo ignorant is he even of the nature of his own countrymen, that he would never imagine the very men he had paid to reſcue the dominions from us, would only conquer to ſeize the ſpoil for themſelves. Such is he whom we now call Nabob; and ſuch are the faithleſs politics of Indoſtan. We have adopted, however, a plan which, if ſtrictly adhered to, muſt effectually prevent his involving the Company, or himſelf, in any difficulties. Mahomed Reza Cawn, Roy Dullub

lub and Juggut Seat, men of the moſt approved credit and moderation, are appointed jointly to the management of all his affairs, nor is either of them to act ſingly in any meaſure of government. The Royal Treaſury is under three different locks and keys, and each of theſe miniſters of ſtate has a key; ſo that no money can be iſſued for any ſervice whatever without the joint knowledge and conſent of them all. Our Reſident at the Durbar is to inſpect the treaſury accounts, from time to time, as he or the Governor and Council may think proper: but we are never to interfere in the appointment or complaints of any officer under the government, nor in any particulars relative to the above-mentioned departments, unleſs ſome extraordinary conduct of the Miniſtry ſhould render alterations requiſite. This form of government I thought proper to recommend, in order to purge the Court of a ſet of knaves and paraſites, by whom the Nabob was ſurrounded, and who were always undermining our influence, that they might the more firmly eſtabliſh their own. So far, you will obſerve, we

have

have exerted ourselves in the arrangement of the Nabob's affairs: but it is a measure of the utmost consequence, since it lays the foundation of that tranquillity, moderation, and regularity which will support the government against any future attempts to a revolution, and we are determined to interest ourselves at the city in no other respect. I need only add, that Mr. Sykes, for whom we intend the residentship, is a gentleman from whose inflexible integrity and long experience in the country politics we have reason to expect the most exact performance of every duty in such an important station.

16th. The regulation of the Nabob's Ministry, the acquisition of the Dewannee, and the honourable terms on which we have concluded a peace with the Vizier of the empire, have placed the dignity and advantages of the English East-India Company on a basis more firm than our most sanguine wishes could a few months ago have suggested. These however alone will not ensure your stability: these are but the outworks which guard you from your natural enemies, the natives of the country: all is not safe: danger still subsists

subsists from more formidable enemies within: luxury, corruption, avarice, rapacity, these have possession of your principal posts, and are ready to betray your citadel. These, therefore, must be extirpated, or they will infallibly destroy us: for we cannot expect the same causes which have ruined the greatest kingdoms should have different effects on such a state as ours. That sudden growth of riches, from whence those evils principally arise, demands our most serious attention. The affairs of Bengal, however glorious and flourishing the prospect may now be, cannot be successfully managed by men whose views extend not above a year or two, and who will set all orders from the Court of Directors at defiance; well knowing they must have acquired an affluent fortune, or at least a comfortable independency, before resentment can reach them. A competency ought to be allowed to all your servants, from the time of their arrival in India; and advantages should gradually increase to each, in proportion to his station: but I would have few of them entertain hopes of returning to their native country till they

they shall have attained the rank of Councillor; then the prospect should open to them, and they should be certain of being enabled to return in a few years with independent fortunes. This certainly would arise from the freight of ships, from the privileges of trade (the advantages of which you are not unacquainted with) and also from the profits upon salt, beetel, and tobacco, agreeable to the new regulation which we have made, in order to rectify the abuses that have been so long committed in those branches of trade; to the great detriment of the country government, without view of benefit to the Company.

17th. The regulation now established for the salt trade will, I hope, be entirely to your satisfaction. I at first intended to propose, that the Company and their servants should be jointly and equally concerned in the trade itself: but, upon better confideration, I judged that plan to be rather unbecoming the dignity of the Company, and concluded it would be better, that they should give the trade entirely to their servants, and fix a duty upon it for themselves equivalent to half the profits. This duty we have computed at the rate of 35 *per cent.* for the prefent; but I imagine it will be able next year to bear an increafe. The articles of beetel and tobacco, being of lefs confequence and yielding much lefs advantage, the duties upon them, of courfe, muft be lefs. For farther particulars of thefe regulations I beg leave to refer you to the Committee letter and proceedings, I would not here trouble you with the repetition of a matter which is there fo fully laid before you.

18th. The advantages propofed for the Governor and Council would undoubtedly appear extremely large to thofe who are unacquainted with the riches of Bengal, and the numberlefs opportunities which the Company's fervants have of acquiring money. But you, who are now perfectly informed of the revenues of thefe kingdoms, and the prodigious emoluments within the reach of gentlemen high in the fervice, will, I am perfuaded, agree with me, that if fome plan of the nature propofed be not adopted, the Governor and Council will not fail to acquire much larger fortunes, by other means

means, in a much shorter time; which must always be productive of that quick succession, not only so detrimental to your commercial interest, but so totally incompatible with the acquisition of political knowledge, which ought now to be considered as a very material qualification in all your civil as well as military servants. To obviate an objection which may arise, that they may possibly proceed in the old way of procuring money, notwithstanding they accept of these allowances, I would have an oath tendered to them, of as strong and solemn a nature as can be penned. I have drawn out the form of one, agreeable to my idea of the expedient, and have the honour to inclose it for your consideration. To this may be annexed a penalty-bond of 150,000 l. to be executed by the Governor, and of 50,000 l. to be executed by each of the Council. Thus the consciences of some will be awakened by the legal consequences of perjury, and pecuniary punishment will be a sure guard over the honesty of others. Could the hearts of men be known by their general character in society, or could their conduct

duct in a state of temptation be ascertained from their moderate attention to wealth whilst the sudden acquisition of it was impossible, the proposal I make would be an affront to religion and morality: but since that is not the case in any part of the world, and least of all so in the East, we must, for our own security, impose such restraints as shall make it impossible even for hypocrisy to introduce corruption.

19th, Having thus fully submitted to you my sentiments on the civil department, permit me to trouble you with a few observations on the military, which deserves a no less serious attention. In the former part of this letter I have mentioned, that luxury and an abhorrence of subordination had overspread your army, but that the good effects of appointing field officers had already become visible. The Committee letter will inclose a general return of their number, and enlarge upon the necessity of keeping each regiment complete to the establishment: I therefore avoid saying any thing here upon those subjects. That letter will also specify the proportion of emolu-

emoluments propoſed for the field officers, from the new acquired advantages upon ſalt. The ſame objection may perhaps be made to this, which I ſuppoſed was likely to occur with reſpect to the plan for the benefit of the civil ſervants. If ſo, I beg leave to refer you to my propoſal and remarks upon that ſubject, which are equally proper and applicable to this. Theſe points then I conclude are ſufficiently before you, and I proceed to recommend to your conſideration, that the regimenting of the troops has introduced a much larger number of officers of rank than has hitherto been admitted upon your eſtabliſhment; and that this regulation, beneficial and neceſſary as it is, will notwithſtanding be productive of one dangerous evil, if not conſtantly guarded againſt by the authority of the Governor and Council, ſupported and enforced by the higher powers at home. The evil I mean to apprize you of, is, the encroachment of the military upon the civil juriſdiction, and an attempt to be independent of their authority. A ſpirit of this kind has always been viſible: our utmoſt vigilance, therefore, is requiſite

to

to suppress it; or at least to take care that it shall not actually prevail. I have been at some pains to inculcate a total subjection of the army to the government, and I doubt not but you will ever maintain that principle. In the field, in time of actual service, I could wish to see the Commander of your forces implicitly relied on for his plan of operations. Orders from the presidency may frequently embarrass him, and prejudice the service. At such a time he is certainly the best judge of what measures should be pursued, and ought, therefore, to be trusted with discretionary powers. But he should by no means be permitted to vary from the fixed general plan of a campaign, nor, from his own idea of the Company's interest, to prosecute operations of importance, when they are not also of real utility and emergency. I dwell not, however, entirely upon the conduct of a Commander of the forces, as such, in the field. He is to understand, that upon all occasions, a gentleman in council is his superior, unless he also has a seat at the Board, and then he will, of course, rank as he stands in that appointment.

ment. The whole army should, in like manner, be subordinate to the civil power; and it is the indispensable duty of the Governor and Council to keep them so. If at any time they should struggle for superiority, the Governor and Council must strenuously exert themselves, ever mindful that they are trustees for the Company in this settlement, and the guardians of public property under a civil institution.

20th. It would give me pain to see a regulation so salutary as that of the appointment of field officers attended with any inconveniencies, and therefore I would earnestly recommend the following very easy and effectual mode of prevention. Let the equality in civil and military rank be immediately settled by the Court of Directors. Were disputes to happen about precedence the only points to be adjusted, they would not be worth a moment's reflection: but we are to consider, that opportunities will sometimes happen when military gentlemen may assume power and authority from the rank they hold among the civil servants, and perhaps pay no attention to orders issued from their

their supposed inferiors. Such contentions may have disagreeable consequences; and to prevent them, I propose, that all the Colonels (the Commander of the troops excepted, who is entitled to the rank of third in council) shall be equal in rank to the Councillors, but always the youngest of that rank. The Lieutenant-colonels should rank with senior merchants, the Majors with junior merchants; Captains with factors, and Lieutenants and Ensigns with writers. The rank of all officers below Colonels, and of civil servants below Councillors, may be considered according to the dates of their commissions and appointments respectively. When such a regulation has taken place, I think the appointment of field officers cannot be charged with a single inconvenience.

21st. Before I quit the subject of the army, I must repeat what, if I mistake not, I mentioned to Mr. Rous before I left England, the propriety of appointing Sir Robert Barker to the command of a regiment, in case of a vacancy. On the death of Colonel Knox I hesitated not to appoint Sir Robert to the third regiment;

but

but it met with opposition, not only from some of the gentlemen in council, but afterwards from Sir Robert Fletcher, who thought himself aggrieved, though at a time when Barker was a Captain he was only a volunteer in your service: and besides Sir Robert Barker must, on all occasions, as the elder officer, have commanded in the field, in the absence of General Carnac and Colonel Smith, even if this appointment had not taken place. If I could imagine that his seniority in the service did not sufficiently intitle him to this preferment, I would urge his experience, which is greater than that of the other gentleman, and his disinterestedness, which made him accept what is ~~most~~ infinitely inferior, in point of emoluments, ~~to~~ the command of the artillery. Lieutenant-colonel Peach has, in like manner, been objected to by the Majors appointed by the Governor and Council: but as it has always been customary to prefer officers of your own appointment to those of the same rank nominated by the Gonor and Council, I need not point out the propriety of your confirming this gentleman's commission. The introducing Lieutenant-colonel Chapman alfo to that rank has met with the fame objections. With regard to him, permit me to acquaint you, that he is a very old Major in the King's fervice, that he was ftrongly folicited at Madrafs to continue there, and on very advantageous terms, when his regiment was ordered home; but that I found him at the Cape, in his way to Europe, and it was with the utmoft difficulty that Meff. Sumner, Sykes and myfelf could prevail upon him to return to India, next in rank to Lieutenant-colonel Peach. His merits on the Coaft have been very great, and I confider him as a very valuable acquifition to your fervice. I therefore moft earneftly requeft you will be pleafed to confirm his appointment as Lieutenant-colonel on this eftablifhment. Neither of thefe three gentlemen I have here fpoken of can be cenfured for that fpirit of licentioufnefs and independency which I have pointed out, as the great evils we ought to guard againft: and the variety, as well as length of their fervices, will certainly be of confiderable advantage to corps like ours. I muft at the fame time confefs, that I cannot be re-

fponfible

sponsible for that discipline and reformation we mean shall take place, unless the field officers are men I can depend upon. Most of the Captains now in your service have had so little experience, and are, I fear, so liable to the general objection, that I could wish to have five or six Captains sent out who have seen service, who understand discipline, and who are well recommended by their Colonels. If you should think proper to extend this plan to Majors, it will be so much the better; but there is no occasion to go higher. Among the appointments you may be pleased to make in England, I could wish to find a majority upon this establishment for Major Pemble, agreeable to the date of the Brevet given him upon his arrival at this place. That gentleman has seen much service, both on the coast of Choromandel, at Manitta, and at Bengal; but being on the Bombay establishment, where the rise is so very slow, he has had the mortification to see himself constantly superseded by the Coast and Bengal officers. You may be assured I would not trouble you with this recommendation, if I did not know him to be worthy of your notice.

22d.

22d. The enquiries I have found myself under the neceffity of promoting, the regulations which I judged proper fhould take place without delay, together with thofe I have here the honour to propofe for your mature deliberation, will, I doubt not, meet with that candid difcuffion which the importance of the fubject requires. You will be pleafed, upon the whole, to obferve, that the great object of my labour has been (and it muft alfo be yours) to ftem that torrent of luxury, corruption, and licentioufnefs which have nearly overwhelmed the intereft, and I might add the exiftence of the Company in thefe parts; to reduce your civil fervants to a fenfe of duty to their employers, and moderation in purfuit of their own advantages; to introduce difcipline, fubordination, and œconomy into your army, and to prevent, in general, that fudden acquifition of riches which is evidently the root of almoft every other evil, both in the civil and military departments.

23d. Is there a man anxious for the fpeedy return of his fon, his brother, or his friend, and folicitous to fee that return

turn accompanied by affluence of fortune, indifferent to the means by which it may have been obtained? Is there who, void of all but selfish feelings, can withhold his approbation of any plan that promises not sudden riches to those of his dearest connections, who can look with contempt upon measures of moderation, and who can cherish all upstart greatness, though stigmatized with the spoils of the Company? If there is such a man, to him all arguments would be vain; to him I speak not. My address is to those who can judge coolly of the advantages to be desired for their relations and friends, nor think the body corporate wholly unentitled to their attention. If these should be of opinion, that an independent fortune honourably acquired, in a faithful service of 12 or 15 years, is more compatible with the interests of the Company than the late rapidity of acquisitions, and at the same time satisfactory to the expectations of reason, I will venture to assert, that the regulations already made, together with those proposed, will, when enforced by the authority of the Court of Directors, ensure to the Company

pany their commercial and political advantages, and be productive of certain independency to every fervant who endeavours to deferve it.

24th. The general terms in which I have mentioned the depravity of this fettlement, oblige me to point out to your attention, the inftances, the very few inftances of diftinguifhed merits among the fuperior fervants. To find a man who, in the midft of luxury and licentioufnefs, had retained the true idea of commercial œconomy; who, inferior in fortune to moft of you civil fervants in the rank of Councillors, was yet fuperior to all in moderation and integrity; whofe regard for the welfare of the public, and for the reputation of individuals, had made him warn others from falling into the temptations of corruption, which he faw were approaching, and who could actually refift thofe temptations himfelf, when a fhare was allotted him of money he thought unwarrantably obtained; to find fuch a man in fuch a fettlement would appear incredible to thofe who are unacquainted with Mr. Verelft. I have reprefented this gentleman to you, as I would

would every one, in his real character: and shall only add, that if you wish to see the measures we are now pursuing supported with integrity, abilities and resolution, you will endeavour to prevail on him to continue in your service, by appointing him to succeed Mr. Sumner in the government. To omit mentioning Mr. Cartier would be injustice, as he also stands high in my opinion. His character is clear: and his attachment to your service what it ought to be, unbiassed by any mean attention to his own advantages. I wish sincerely your list of superior servants would enable me to detain you longer on subjects of commendation: but I have finished the picture, and cannot add another figure that deserves to be distinguished from the groupe.

25th. Having filled so many pages upon the subject of public affairs, you will indulge me with a few lines upon a circumstance which concerns myself. Mr. Johnstone, in his last minute in council, has thought proper to throw out some observations upon the validity of my title to the jaghire, insinuating that the defect which he pretends to have discovered was not known at the time of my litigation with the Company. As I would not wish that a point in which my honour is concerned should pass unnoticed, I must observe, that the King's funnud, which Mr. Johnstone affirmed was requisite to be attained within 6 months from the granting of the jaghire for the conformation of it, is a matter of form only, and not understood to be essential. As a proof of this, I inclose translations of various jaghire grants, properly attested by Mr. Vansittart, the Persian translator; as also an attestation of the same gentleman, that the grant to me was as complete as other grants of that nature generally are: but to put this matter out of dispute, the paper of agreement which Mr. Johnstone alludes to, is of no more consequence than a piece of blank paper, since it was never executed by me, or by any agent, or vaquiel on my account; nor was any agent ever named, or thought of by me. Inclosed, I transmit you a translation of the very paper, attested also by Mr. Vansittart.

26th, Permit me now to remind you that I have a large family who stand in need of a father's protection; that I sacrifice

fice my health and hazard my fortune, with my life, by continuing in this climate. The first great purposes of my appointment are perfectly answered: peace is restored, and my engagement to procure for the Company the reversion of my jaghire is completed in the fullest manner, since it is not only confirmed by the present Nabob, but by the Great Mogul. I now only wait to be informed whether my conduct thus far be approved of, and whether the whole, or any part of the regulations I have had the honour to lay before you are conformable to your ideas of the reformation necessary to be established. If they meet with your approbation, I doubt not you will immediately empower me, in conjunction with the Select Committee, to finish the business so successfully begun; which may easily be effected before the end of the ensuing year, when I am determined to return to Europe, and hope to acquaint you in person with the accomplishment of every wish you can form for the prosperity of your affairs in Bengal.

27th. I shall conclude this tedious letter by observing, that my anxiety to know

know whether you approve of my conduct, or not, can proceed from no other motive than my concern for the public; since I continue invariable in the refolution I formed and expreffed in a General Court, long before the covenants were propofed, of acquiring no addition to my fortune by my acceptance of the government: and I beg leave alfo to affure you, that in order to obviate all fufpicion of a collufion in this delicate point, I have not permitted either of the gentlemen of my family to hold an employment in your fervice, nor to receive prefents, although they are not bound by covenants to the contrary. The fmall congratulatory nazurs, elephants, horfes, &c. which I have been under a neceffity of receiving, do not, I imagine, amount to any confiderable fum; but whatever it may be, not a farthing fhall go into my own pocket. I have hitherto been too much engaged in matters of public importance to attend to a particular valuation; but I have caufed an exact account to be kept of every, even the moft trifling prefent, which at my return fhall be fubmitted to your infpection: and in

the

the mean time, the amount of the whole shall go towards defraying my extraordinary expences, as Governor. The only favour I have to solicit for myself is, that although your treasury here will for the future be so full as to render it difficult for individuals to obtain bills upon the Company, payable at home, you will be pleased to indulge me with the usual channel of remittance of my jaghire, untill it reverts to the Company.

I have the honour to be, with the utmost respect,

GENTLEMEN,

Your most obedient and

most humble servant,

(Signed) CLIVE.

To the Honourable the COURT of DIRECTORS.

28th. I cannot help requesting your attention to Mr. William Wynne, a young gentleman whom I brought out to India with me, and whom I was in hopes of seeing

seeing appointed a writer on the list of that year. I have caused him to transcribe this letter, that you may see he is qualified in point of penmanship; and as he has lived constantly with me, and acted as assistant to my secretary, I can take upon me to be responsible for his conduct and abilities in every respect. It is, therefore, my particular request, that you confer on him the station of a writer, to take rank from the time of his leaving England.

29th. I beg leave also to recommend to your protection Mr. Maddison, a gentleman of a liberal education, and who promises to be a very valuable servant to the Company, from an uncommon facility in acquiring the Persian language. As he is 27 years of age, you will not think me unreasonable in soliciting for him the appointment of a factor.

(Signed) CLIVE.

COPY OF A LETTER

FROM

THE RIGHT HON. LORD CLIVE,

And the Rest of the SELECT COMMITEE, at FORT WILLIAM, in BENGAL,

TO THE

COURT OF DIRECTORS

OF THE EAST-INDIA COMPANY.

[Dated the 30th September 1765.]

GENTLEMEN,

1st. THE accompanying proceedings of the Select Committee will explain our motives for purchasing the Admiral Stevens to convey to your hands these dispaches, which we hope will be deemed of sufficient importance to merit any extraordinary expence thereby incurred; an expence which we flatter ourselves

selves will be fully defrayed by the valuable cargo which she carries home at this early season.

2d. By the general letter of this date you will be informed, by the President and Council, of every material concern that has been transacted before the Board. At the same time, we beg leave to refer to the letters dispatched by the Vansittart and Bute (whereof duplicates are now inclosed) for a detail of the military operations, political occurrences, and especially the very important transactions previous to our arrival, and subsequent to the death of Meer Jaffier. An event that furnished the most glorious opportunity of establishing your influence and power on so solid a basis, as must soon have rendered the English East-India Company the most potent commercial body that ever flourished at any period of time.

3d. It is from a due sense of the regard we owe and profess to your interest, and to our own honour, that we think it indispensably necessary to lay open to your view a series of transactions too notoriously known to be suppressed, and too affecting to your interest, to the national character,

character, and to the existence of the Company in Bengal, to escape unnoticed and uncensured: transactions which seem to demonstrate, that every spring of this government was smeared with corruption; that principles of rapacity and oppression universally prevailed, and that every spark of sentiment and public spirit was lost and extinguished in the unbounded lust of unmerited wealth.

4th. To illustrate these positions, we must exhibit to your view a most unpleasing variety of complaints, inquiries, evidences, accusations and vindications, the particulars of which are entered in our proceedings and the appendix; assuring you, that we undertake this task with peculiar reluctance, from the personal regard we entertain for some of the gentlemen whose characters will appear to be deeply affected.

5th. At Fort St. George, we received the first advices of the demise of Meer Jaffier, and of Shujah Dowlah's defeat. It was there firmly imagined, that no definitive measures would be taken, either in respect to a peace, or filling the vacancy in the Nizamut, before our arrival, as the

H   Lapwing

Lapwing arrived in the month of January with your general letter, and the appointment of a Committee, with express powers to that purpose, for the successful exertion of which the happiest occasion now offered. However a contrary resolution prevailed in the Council. The opportunity of acquiring immense fortunes was too inviting to be neglected, and the temptation too powerful to be resisted. A treaty was hastily drawn up by the Board, or rather transcribed, with a few unimportant additions, from that concluded with Meer Jaffier; and a deputation, consisting of Messieurs Johnstone, Senior, Middleton and Leycester, appointed to raise the natural son of the deceased Nabob to the Subahdarry, in prejudice of the claim of the grandson; and for this measure such reasons are assigned as ought to have dictated a diametrically opposite resolution. Miran's son was a minor: which circumstance alone would have naturally brought the whole administration into our hands, at a juncture when it became indispensably necessary we should realize that shadow of power and influence which, having no solid foundation,

tion, was expofed to the danger of being annihilated by the firft ftroke of adverfe fortune. But this inconfiftency was not regarded, nor was it material to the views for precipitating the treaty which was preffed on the young Nabob, at the firft view, in fo earneft and indelicate a manner as highly difgufted him and chagrined his minifters; while not a fingle rupee was ftipulated for the Company, whofe interefts were facrificed, that their fervants might revel in the fpoils of a treafury before impoverifhed, but now totally exhaufted.

6th. This fcene of corruption was firft difclofed at a vifit the Nabob paid to Lord Clive and the gentlemen of the Committee, a few days after our arrival. He there delivered to his Lordfhip a letter, filled with bitter complaints of the infults and indignities he had been expofed to, and the embezzlement of near twenty laaks of rupees, iffued from his treafury, for purpofes unknown, during the late negotiations. So public a complaint could not be difregarded: and it foon produced an enquiry. We referred the letter to the Board, in expectation of obtaining

taining a satisfactory account of the application of this money; and were answered only by a warm remonstrance, entered by Mr. Leycester, against that very Nabob in whose elevation he boasts of having been a principal agent.

7th. Mahomed Reza Cawn, the Naib Subah, was then called upon to account for this large disbursement from the treasury: and he soon delivered to the Committee the very extraordinary narrative entered in our proceedings of the 6th June, wherein he specifies the several names, the sums by whom paid, and to whom, whether in bills, cash, or obligations. So precise, so accurate an account as this, of money issued for secret and venal services, was never, we believe, before this period exhibited to the honourable Court of Directors; at least never vouched by such undeniable testimony, and authentic documents; by Juggut Seat, who himself was obliged to contribute largely to the sums demanded by Mootyram, who was employed by Mr. Johnstone in all these pecuniary transactions; by the Nabob, and Mahomed Reza Cawn, who were the heaviest sufferers, and,

and, lastly, by the confession of the gentlemen themselves, whose names are specified in the distribution list.

8th. Juggut Seat expresly declares, in his narrative, that the sum which he agreed to pay the deputation, amounting to 125,000 rupees, was extorted by menaces; and since the close of our enquiry, and the opinions we delivered in the proceedings of the 21st June, it fully appears, that the presents from the Nabob and Mahomed Reza Cawn, exceeding the immense sum of seventeen laaks, were not the voluntary offerings of gratitude, but contributions levied on the weakness of the government, and violently exacted from the dependent state and timid disposition of the minister. The charge indeed is denied on the one hand, as well as affirmed on the other. Your honourable Board must, therefore, determine how far the circumstance of extortion may aggravate the crime of disobedience to your positive orders, the exposing the government in a manner to sale, and receiving the infamous wages of corruption from opposite parties and contending interests. We speak with boldness, because

we

we speak from conviction founded upon indubitable facts, that besides the above sums, specified in the distribution account to the amount of 228,125 l. sterling, there was likewise to the value of several laaks of rupees procured from Nundcomar and Roydullub, each of whom aspired at, and obtained a promise of that very employment that was predetermined to be bestowed on Mahomed Reza Cawn. The particulars of this extraordinary bargain came too late to our hands to be inserted in the proceedings; nor do we think it material, since to insist on farther proofs than are already fully and clearly exhibited, in order to convince you that our enquiry was necessary and our decision moderate, would, we apprehend, serve rather to exhaust your patience than confirm your belief.

9th. These particulars being submitted to your consideration, it may be necessary to offer a few remarks on the arguments urged by these gentlemen in their several minutes, either in their own justification, or with a view that our proceedings should appear arbitrary and oppressive. Mess. Johnstone, Senior, Leycester, Burdett

Burdett and Gray vindicate the receiving of presents by arguments which, in our opinion, render their conduct still more culpable. They urge, that as the covenants were not then executed, they could not be obligatory. In answer, we will beg leave to ask those gentlemen, whether the Company's orders were not then received? Whether the intention and spirit of those orders were not clearly and perfectly understood? Whether the covenants themselves were not transmitted from England, ready to be filled up and executed? Whether a single motion for fulfilling the Company's instructions appears on the face of the consultations? Whether it was not incumbent on them, as the superior power, to set this example of respect and deference to the orders of their constituents? And whether they conceive the Company would have sustained any detriment by this act of their obedience? How then came the orders to be totally neglected, at a juncture especially when the letter and spirit of those obligations clearly manifested that particular regard should be had to their execution?

10th,

10th. The same gentlemen arraign the conduct, and even deny the powers of the Select Committee. Mr. Leycester, in particular, affirms, that candor and decency required the truth of a charge brought against any of the members of the Board, should be determined by the Board. You, gentlemen, will be able to judge of the force of this argument, and of the propriety of the measure proposed, when we acquaint you, that of a Board then sitting of the presidency, consisting of the president and eight members, five of those members were themselves the accused, who, by having a majority of voices, would of consequence become the judges of their own conduct. We will not enter into a discussion of the precise powers entrusted to the Committee; but we may venture to affirm, that unless the spirit of their instructions be extended to the correction of abuses, the detection of corruption, and the punishment of disobedience, the ends proposed of restoring peace and tranquillity will be frustrated, and their appointment rendered ridiculous and absurd.

Mr.

11th. Mr. Johnstone is pleased to assert, that no proofs can be produced of menaces being used to obtain a sum of money from Juggut Seat. To this we reply, by a reference to the evidence of his own agent, Mootyram, where it is declared upon oath, that he delivered by Mr. Johnstone's express orders the very messages recited in his examination. Messages of such tendency as certainly would bear hard on Mr. Johnstone's character. As to what he further adds, of our obtaining this evidence by military force and terrors, we are sorry to see a gentleman reduced to the necessity of resting his defence on the subterfuge of a pitiful evasion. Mr. Johnstone certainly knows, at least he ought to know as the proceedings were immediately sent to him, that Mootyram was seized in the commission of a clandestine, illegal act, of interesting consequence to the public in general, and to Mr. Johnstone and the gentlemen of the deputation in particular. Mootyram was actually detected in an attempt to suppress bills, to the amount of 475,000 rupees, which had been wrongfully obtained from Mahomed Reza Cawn, and screen from discovery a circumstance which it highly imported the Committee to know; and which Mr. Johnstone should have made known, were he solicitous to exculpate himself from a charge that deeply affected his reputation, and of such irreproachable conduct as he would endeavour to persuade the world to believe. But that not the least shadow of a doubt might remain of the candour and equity of the measures we pursued, we readily consented that the same Mootyram might be re-examined in the presence of the Council; where he confirmed, without contradiction or evasion, every material circumstance set forth in his first evidence. The remainder of Mr. Johnstone's minute, you will perceive, doth not affect the Committee as a body. It consists entirely of personal invective, loose and virulent declamation, the genuine effects of enraged disappointment and detection. Yet should any thing further be required in answer, we beg leave to refer you to the replies made by Lord CLIVE, and the Members of the Committee, which we flatter ourselves will appear full and explicit.

12th.

12th. One circumstance more occurs in the course of these gentlemens' minutes that merits our observation. It is declared by Mr. Leycester, upon oath, that he did not receive the present intended him by Mahomed Reza Cawn, and that his letters will demonstrate his intention was to have refused it. This is a fact, of the truth of which we entertain not the least doubt; but it proves nothing more than that Mr. Leycester would not receive a sum of money after the covenants had been enforced by the Committee, and an enquiry set on foot concerning the distribution of that very money; a part of which was now privately tendered back to Mahomed Reza Cawn. He will not deny, that he knew of the intended present when he was at Cossimbuzar: the letters of Messrs. Senior and Middleton prove that he did. He will not deny, that bills to the amount of 50,000 rupees were made out in his name: their being offered back to Mahomed Reza Cawn, and Mootyram's being detected in the fact evince it. The whole, therefore, of this solemn asseveration amounts only to an evasion in respect

spect to time and circumstances, which no way affect the nature of the act itself.

13th. Having now explained the origin and progress of this disagreeable enquiry, we beg leave to touch upon a few circumstances in justification of the lenity of our opinions delivered, and resolutions entered in the Committee proceedings of the 21st of June. And here we must observe, that notwithstanding we believed a reformation of abuses to be actually our duty, yet we could not think the same duty necessarily extended to the punishment of transgressions. We owed a regard to the persons and characters of some of the gentlemen concerned, who must suffer extremely by a suspension, or dismission. The great objects of our wishes were, that your service might in future be conducted with integrity, diligence and œconomy, without a retrospect to the past, where it could be avoided. The subject indeed of the present enquiry was so recent, it was of so interesting a nature to the public, and came recommended to us, or rather was forced upon us, with such peculiar circumstances as rendered our proceeding to a scrutiny necessary

necessary to our reputation; but the severity of judgment, and a decision which would have left so great a void in your Council, was not equally necessary either to your interest or to our honour. Such an event might have impressed the minds of the natives with strange ideas of the fluctuating situation of our Councils: and it would unvoidably have admitted a number of your junior servants to the supreme direction of this vast machine of government, at an age little exceeding that period fixed by the laws of their country for entrusting them with the management of their own private fortunes. We must farther observe, that many of the most aggravating circumstances had not then reached our knowledge; at the same time we were under the necessity of coming to some determination. Shujah Dowlah impatiently expected Lord Clive in camp, to conclude the proposed treaty and the regulations of the government lately established; and other matters, then transacting, absolutely required Mr. Sykes's attendance at the Durbar. Some of the extraordinary facts above related were obtained since their

their departure; and had they come sooner, they would have served only to perplex and embarrass us the more. In a word, to obviate future evils we considered as our immediate duty, the punishment of past misconduct we chose to refer to your honourable Board, that malice itself should have no foundation for asserting, that we had assumed and exerted a power not fully and expresly authorized by the Court of Directors. We think it necessary to declare, in justice to Mr. Cartier, that his character stands irreproachable in the list of your servants; that he never knew of, or consented to the receiving any the smallest present, either from the Nabob, or from Mahomed Reza Cawn.

14th. Although we will not take upon us to declare, that we entirely approve of the covenants, in the form in which they have been transmitted, yet we are persuaded, from the instances just related, that some restraint is necessary to prevent the abuse of the customary indulgence to receive presents: this indulgence has certainly been extended to the most shameful oppression and flagrant corruption,

and

and is otherwife attended with manifold inconveniencies to the fervice. We, therefore, determined immediately to enforce your inftructions, relative to thofe obligations; and to bind down by laws all fuch as are not to be checked by a fenfe of honour and juftice: you will accordingly obferve, that carrying thofe orders into ftrict execution, throughout every department, civil and military, was among the earlieft tranfactions of your Select Committee.

15th. We alfo took an early opportunity of confidering the tendency of your repeated inftructions for recalling free merchants and other Europeans, who without the leaft claim to your protection from indentures, were neverthelefs permitted to refide up the country, and in all the different parts of the Nabob's dominions. Sorry we are to obferve, that this indulgence has frequently given birth to grievous acts of infult and oppreffion at places remote from the prefidency and fubordinate factories, and that carrying your orders into execution becomes daily more neceffary. By this meafure, however, the bufinefs of your fervants will fuffer

con-

confiderably, from their being now obliged to employ black Gomaftahs on many affairs that demand the vigour and activity of Europeans. Hence likewife will many perfons of real merit be deprived of the means of fubfiftence: yet, in confideration that private intereft muft give way to public benefit, and that it is our duty to obey where your immediate interefts do not abfolutely require a deviation from your orders, we determined to recall all the Europeans refiding up the country under protection of the Englifh name, by the 21ft day of October next, and have for that purpofe circulated advertifements and orders to the different fubordinates.

16th. Regulating the country government was the next object of your attention. We found the Nabob highly diffatiffied with the plenary powers vefted in Mahomed Reza Cawn, who, by virtue of the treaty, acted in quality of prime Minifter, and enjoyed uncontrouled authority. This unlimited fway, lodged in the hands of a fingle perfon, appeared dangerous to the prefent eftablifhment; which we thought it becoming the Company's honour to maintain, as having

been

been solemnly ratified by the Governor and Council. To amend the very obvious defects in the treaty, without oversetting the principles on which it was founded, was consistent with equity, while it met with the Nabob's own approbation. And the most effectual means of doing this seemed, to us, to consist in an equal partition of ministerial influence. As Mahomed Reza Cawn's short administration was irreproachable, we determined to continue him in a share of the authority, at the same time that we associated with him men of weight and character; so that each became a check on the conduct of the others. Accordingly we fixed on Juggut Seat and Roydullub, for the reasons assigned in the proceedings, and we now have the pleasure to acquaint you, that the business of the government goes on with unanimity, vigour and dispatch.

17th. By the last dispatches you were advised, that Shujah Dowlah was making fresh and formidable preparations to penetrate a second time into the Nabob's Dominions. He had found means to engage Mulhar, a considerable Marattah Chief,

Chief, in his alliance; and if the judicious and vigorous meafures purfued by General Carnac had not prevented a junction of the numerous forces deftined for this invafion, a ruinous war muft have been fupported through the courfe of another campaign. The enemy's fituation rendered their defign for fome time uncertain, and obliged the General to great circumfpection in his movements, left he fhould leave the frontiers expofed. Having, however, at length received undoubted advice they had taken the Korah Road, he fufpected their intention was to fall upon Sir Robert Fletcher, who commanded a feparate corps in that diftrict. Accordingly he made fome forced marches to effect a junction, which he happily accomplifhed, and then the united army moved in purfuit of the enemy. On the 3d day of May the General came up with, attacked and entirely defeated them: in confequence of which Shujah Dowlah feparated from his allies, while the Marattahs retired with precipitation towards the Jumna. In fact, this blow appears to have been decifive; for Shujah Dowlah never again attempted to join the Marattahs,

tahs, who obferving the General dropt the purfuit, in order to watch the Vizier, made a fecond effort to re-enter Korah, in which they were difappointed. Perfuaded that, to ftop their incurfions, it would be neceffary to drive them beyond the Jumna, the General croffed the river the 22d, diflodged them from their poft on the oppofite fide, and obliged them to retire to the hills. Here he quitted his purfuit, and returned to his ftation at Jafmall, to receive Shujah Dowlah, who had intimated a defire of fubmitting to whatever conditions we fhould think fit to prefcribe. His letter to the General expreffes his feelings: and the reception he met with in our camp was fuch as policy dictated fhould be given to a vanquifhed enemy of Shujah Dowlah's rank and character.

18th. A peace with the Vizier became the next immediate object of our deliberations: in adjufting which we endeavoured to extend our views beyond the prefent advantages that might poffibly be obtained. We regarded Shujah Dowlah's perfonal character, and high reputation over the whole empire; the fituation of his coun-try,

try, which we had conquered, and the great riſk and expence of maintaining this conqueſt if we cloſed in with the plan adopted by the late Governor and Council, of giving it up to Nadjuff Cawn; who had neither weight of reputation, nor of force ſufficient to keep poſſeſſion, nor to form a ſecure barrier to the Nabob's dominions. The words of our inſtructions to Lord Clive, when he left the preſidency to adjuſt the conditions of a peace, expreſs the ſentiments which we ſtill entertain on this ſubject. " Experience hav-
" ing ſhewn, that an influence obtained
" by force of arms is deſtructive of that
" commercial ſpirit which we ought to
" promote, ruinous to the Company and
" oppreſſive to the country, we earneſtly
" recommend to your Lordſhip, that you
" will exert your utmoſt endeavours to
" to conciliate the affections of the coun-
" try powers, to remove any jealouſy they
" may entertain of our unbounded ambition, and to convince them we aim
" not at conqueſt and dominion, but
" ſecurity in carrying on a free trade,
" equally beneficial to them and to us.

" With

" With this view, policy requires that
" our demands be moderate and equita-
" ble, and that we avoid every appear-
" ance of an inclination to enlarge our
" territorial poffeffions. The facrifice of
" conquefts which we muft hold on a very
" precarious tenure, and at an expence
" more than equivalent to their revenues,
" is of little confequence to us; yet will
" fuch reftitution imprefs them with an
" high opinion of our generofity and
" juftice.

" For thefe reafons, we think Shujah
" Dowlah fhould be reinftated in the full
" poffeffion of all his dominions, with
" fuch limitations only as he muft fee are
" evidently calculated for our mutual
" benefit. We would decline infifting
" upon any terms that muft prove irk-
" fome to his high fpirit, and imply a
" fufpicion of his fincerity. Retaining
" poffeffion of any of his high holds may
" poffibly be deemed a neceffary pledge
" of his fidelity: for our parts, we would
" rather confider it as the fource of fu-
" ture contention, and an unneceffary
" burthen to the Company, unlefs it be
" one day propofed to refume the thoughts
" of

" of extending their dominions, a mea-
" fure very oppofite to the fentiments in
" which we left the Court of Directors."

19th. Agreeable to thefe inftructions, his Lordfhip and General Carnac concluded a treaty of peace with Shujah Dowlah, that will, if any thing can, fecure his friendfhip and fidelity, and render the public tranquillity permanent. They found him extremely averfe to the eftablifhment of factories in his dominions, which he confidered as laying the foundation of a future rupture, and the only thing that could poffibly difturb our amity. He very juftly obferved, that our encroachments in Bengal, the great abufes of the Company's fervants, and extraordinary extenfion of the privileges originally granted to the Englifh, had been productive of much confufion and bloodfhed in Bengal, and he feared might produce fimilar confequences in his country. Accordingly Lord Clive and General Carnac judged it advifeable to omit the word *Factories* in the treaty, but without relinquifhing the right, fhould it be found expedient after mature deliberation to enforce it. To fpeak our fentiments free-

ly,

ly, we can forefee no benefit that can arife to the Company from maintaining fettlements at fo vaft a diftance from the prefidency, whatever advantages may arife to their fervants ; at leaft the profpect is fo remote, while the expences are fo certain, the rifk fo evident, and the difputes it will occafion fo probable, that we are at prefent of opinion, that the factory lately eftablifhed at Benaris ought immediately to be withdrawn, we mean as foon as the agreement between the Company and Bulwantfing is expired. The limits of the Nabob's dominions are fufficient to anfwer all your purpofes. Thefe, we think, ought to conftitute the boundaries, not only of all your territorial poffeffions and influence in thefe parts, but of your commerce alfo ; since by grafping at more you endanger the fafety of thofe immenfe revenues, and that well-founded power which you now enjoy, without the hope of obtaining an adequate advantage.

20th. With refpect to the other articles of the treaty, you will obferve, that a fufficient provifion is fecured for the fupport of the King's honour and dignity, without

out danger of his becoming a future incumbrance; and that twenty-six laaks yearly are granted to him on the revenues of Bengal, a revenue far more considerable than he ever before enjoyed. In gratitude for this inftance of our attention to his intereft, his Majefty has been pleafed to beftow on the Company the moft important grants ever yet obtained by any European ftate from the Mogul Court. Befides confirming to the Company all their former poffeffions, and fecuring to them the reverfion in perpetuity of Lord Clive's Jaghire, he has conferred on them the Dewannee of Bengal, Bahar and Orixa, and ratified, in the ftrongeft terms, an agreement we propofed concluding with the Nabob, if the King's confent could be procured; fubjects which it will be neceffary to explain in a feparate paragraph. Another article ftipulates, that Shujah Dowlah fhall pay the Company fifty laaks of rupees, by way of indemnification for the charges incurred by the war. This indemnification we know inadequate: but his circumftances would not afford more, without oppreffing the country, and thereby laying

ing the foundation of future contention and trouble; and accordingly you will perceive that no money is granted for any other confideration whatever. As to furrendering Coffim Ally, Sombre and the deferters, complying with fuch a demand is now utterly out of his power. The former we hear has fought fhelter in the Rohillah country, and the latter refide under the protection of the Jauts, fcreened both from Shujah Dowlah and from us; fo that making this an effential preliminary would be highly unreafonable and abfurd. However it is ftipulated, that they fhall never meet with encouragement or affiftance from Shujah Dowlah, or be ever again admitted into his country. Upon the whole, we have paid fuch regard to Shujah Dowlah's character and intereft, and to what juftice as well as policy requires, without any the fmalleft facrifice of your honour or intereft, that we entertain the moft flattering hope this treaty of peace will be lafting, and our frontiers on that quarter perfectly fecure againft future invafions.

21ft. The time now approaches when we may be able to determine, with fome

L   degree

degree of certainty, whether our remaining as merchants, subjected to the jurisdiction, encroachments and insults of the country government, or the supporting your privileges and possessions by the sword, are likely to prove most beneficial to the Company. Whatever may be the consequence, certain it is, that after having once begun and proceeded to such lengths as we have been forced to go, from step to step, until your whole possessions were put to the risk by every revolution effected, and every battle fought, to apply a remedy to these evils, by giving stability and permanency to your government, is now and has been the constant object of the the serious attention of your Select Committee.

22d. The perpetual struggles for superiority between the Nabob's and your agents, together with the recent proofs before us of notorious and avowed corruption, have rendered us unanimously of opinion, after the most mature deliberation, that no other method could be suggested of laying the axe to the root of all these evils, than that of obtaining the Dewannee of Bengal, Bahar and Orixa for

the

the Company. By establishing the power of the Great Mogul, we have likewise established his rights: and his Majesty, from principles of gratitude, equity and policy, has thought proper to bestow this important employment on the Company; the nature of which is, the collecting of all the revenues, and after defraying the expences of the army, and allowing a sufficient fund for the support of the Nizamut, to remit the remainder to Delhi, or wherever the King shall reside, or direct. But as the King has been graciously pleased to bestow on the Company for ever, such surplus as shall arise from the revenues, upon certain stipulations and agreements expressed in the Sunnud, we have settled with the Nabob, with his own free will and consent, that the sum of fifty-three laaks shall be annually paid to him for the support of his dignity, and all contingent expences, exclusive of the charge of maintaining an army, which is to be defrayed out of the revenues ceded to the Company by this royal grant of the Dewannee; and indeed the Nabob has abundant reason to be well satisfied with the conditions of his agreement,

whereby

whereby a fund is secured to him, without trouble or danger, adequate to all the purposes of such grandeur and happiness as a man of his sentiments has any conception of enjoying. More would serve only to disturb his quiet, endanger his government and sap the foundation of that solid structure of power and wealth which, at length, is happily reared and compleated by the Company, after a vast expence of blood and treasure.

23d. By this acquisition of the Dewannee, your possessions and influence are rendered permanent and secure; since no future Nabob will either have power or riches sufficient to attempt your overthrow by means either of force or corruption. All revolutions must hence forward be at an end, as there will be no fund for secret services, for donations, or for restitutions. The Nabob cannot answer the expectations of the venal and mercenary, nor will the Company comply with demands injurious to themselves, out of their own revenues. The experience of years has convinced us, that a division of power is impossible, without generating discontent, and hazarding the whole.

whole. All must belong either to the Company or to the Nabob: and we leave you to judge which alternative is the most desirable, and the most expedient in the present circumstances of affairs. As to ourselves, we know of no system we could adopt, that would less affect the Nabob's dignity, and at the same time secure the Company against the fatal effects of future revolutions, than this of the Dewannee. The power is now lodged where it can only be lodged with safety to us; so that we may pronounce, with some degree of confidence, that the worst that will happen in future to the Company will proceed from temporary ravages only; which can never become so general as to prevent your revenues from yielding a sufficient fund to defray your civil and military charges, and furnish your investments.

24th. But to secure these valuable possessions, a constant regard must be paid to your military establishment. By the regimental returns which we inclose in the packet, and which are very exact, you will see at one view the deplorable condition of our infantry; to complete which,

which, agreeable to your directions and to the proposal made by Lord Clive, not less than nine hundred men will suffice. We therefore most earnestly request, that you will next year send out twelve or fourteen hundred men for this establishment; giving such peremptory orders as must be obeyed, that none of this number be detained upon any consideration on the coast of Choromandel. Our numbers once completed, we shall require, for the security of your immense possessions in this country, not more than six hundred recruits to be sent out annually in the following manner, viz. five hundred infantry, sixty artillery, twenty cavalry, and twenty serjeants for the Seapoys. To this number must be added thirty volunteers and officers; and it would be of the utmost benefit to our plan, that you send out every year six or seven gentlemen from the Academy at Woolwich, for artillery officers; this being a service that suffers extremely for want of persons properly instructed to conduct it, since no officer who knows the benefit of the infantry service here will chuse to quit it for any advantage the artillery will afford.

25th

25th. Already we feel the good effects of regimenting your troops. Discipline, subordination and œconomy begin to to take place. Had General Carnac's merit been much greater, if possible, than it is, he could not effect this of himself, unassisted as he was by field officers, and thwarted as he always has been by the late Governors and Councils. We have already issued our orders for striking off half the double Batta, and shall in a very few days put your forces entirely upon a footing with the troops on the coast of Choromandel; which will be reducing your military expences as low as they can well bear, consistently with your interest and the good of the service.

26th. Before we quit this subject, we must request in the strongest manner, you will supply us, for the first year, with 10,000 stands of small arms, and afterwards with 4000 annually; which will in future answer all our demands, if proper care be taken in the purchase. Of late years, the bad quality of your small arms in general has exposed your possessions to the greatest risk and danger. The locks are ill finished, and

the

the metal so badly tempered, as not to stand the heat of the sun in this climate. We are, therefore, persuaded it would prove in the end much to your advantage, if you purchased all your small arms of the same persons who furnish the government, and pay at the rate of twenty-seven, instead of eighteen shillings *per firelock*; since experience demonstrates they will continue serviceable for double the time, without being liable to the inconveniencies above represented. The iron-founder, whom you sent out in the Kent, died on his passage to this place; but as the casting of shot and shells in this country is an object of great importance, we strongly recommend that you will supply the loss as soon as possible, by sending three or four persons well versed in that business, that our whole design may not be frustrated by such an accident in future. It also merits your serious consideration to provide, by every possible means, against the illicit importation of small arms to your settlements in India, and particularly Bengal. Of late years this was become a profitable branch of trade with the Europe Captains, as well

as

as that of furnishing the natives with ammunition; and they elude the searches of your officers by sending round small vessels to meet them at sea, in certain latitudes, or to Teneriff and St. Jago, or elsewhere, out of the reach of your enquiries. However, as their continuing such practices any longer may prove fatal in their consequences to all your possessions in this country, we earnestly exhort, that you will immediately apply the most effectual remedy you can suggest, either by way of prevention, or by the rigorous and exemplary punishment of the offenders. At the same time, you may depend we will take every step in our power to detect the least breach of your orders on this head, and obstruct the sale of all kinds of fire-arms.

27th. Having observed the reluctance that appeared in bidding for your farms at the last sale of your lands in Burdwan province, the great annual deficiency in the collections, and the numberless complaints made of grievous exactions and oppressions; we determined, upon Mr. Johnstone's resigning your service, to appoint Mr. Verelst in quality of supervisor of those revenues; in order to form the best judgment possible of the cause of this yearly deficiency of the real value of the lands, the best method of improving and letting them, and also to procure the necessary materials for a plan to conduct the collections, in future, in such manner as shall appear most conducive to your interest, and likely to promote the happiness of the people, It is with pleasure we acquaint you, that we have the greatest reason to be satisfied with Mr. Verelst's attention to the several objects recommended, and the diligence he has exerted during his short residence in that country; of which you may form some judgment from his memorial to the Committee, annexed to our proceedings of the 14th of September.

28th. It was in consequence of this memorial that we formed our resolution, of that date, to withdraw the factory; and also to recal the Member of the Board resident at Midnapoor, the collections and business of which may as conveniently be transacted by a junior servant, at a much less expence. Many are the inconveniencies, besides the extraordinary charge incurred,

incurred, that refult from fuch appointments; which we confider as neceffary only at thofe fubordinates where your principle inveftments are made. We are convinced, by very late experience, that the moft flagrant oppreffions may be wantonly committed in thofe employments, by Members of the Board, which would not be tolerated in junior fervants: and that the dread and awe annexed to their ftation, as Councillors, has too frequently fcreened them from complaints, which would be lodged without fear or fcruple againft junior fervants.

29th. But there are other manifold inconveniencies, of ftill more pernicious effect to the fervice, that refult from thofe appointments. Hence it was found neceffary to enlarge the Council from twelve to fixteen Members, that there might be a fufficient number to conduct the bufinefs of the prefidency, and alfo to manage your affairs at the out fettlements, either in quality of Chiefs, or Refidents. What is the confequence, but fuch perpetual changes and revolutions at the Board as render it impoffible for any of the Members to acquire a competent knowledge of of your interests, and of the particular duty of their own station? This increase in the number of the Board is also productive of a further inconvenience, of the deepest concern to your interest in the present situation of your affairs. To keep up to the letter of your instructions, we must fill the vacancies in Council from the next in succession, without regard to the qualifications they possess for the discharge of so important a trust; and thus commit into the hands of rash, inexperienced and ignorant young men the conduct of a system of government which demands the discretion, judgment and steadiness of more advanced years, and longer services. Circumstances are now widely different from what they were a few years since, when you confined your whole attention to commerce, and were happy in being able to complete your investments, without insult or exaction from the country governments. *You are now become the Sovereigns of a rich and potent kingdom.* Your success is beheld with jealousy by the other European nations who maintain settlements in India: and your interests are so extended, so complicated,

cated, and so connected with those of the several surrounding powers, as to form a nice and difficult system of politicks.

30th. These weighty considerations determined us to avoid filling the vacancies lately occasioned in Council, by the death of Mr. Billers and resignation of Messrs. Johnstone and Burdett. We carefully examined your orders respecting the appointment of a Board. We compared the different paragraphs of your letter, the more clearly to ascertain the spirit of your instructions: and are unanimous in our opinion, that your reasons for increasing the number of the Board were founded on a supposition, that this measure would conduce to the benefit of the Company. Experience convinces us of the contrary: and we should be wanting in duty to our constituents, if, from a servile regard to the letter, we neglected the evident sense and meaning of your instructions, by admitting to the government of your affairs a number of persons who have certainly no other claim to this distinction than that of standing next in succession. It is with the utmost regret we think it

incum-

incumbent on us to declare, that in the whole lift of your junior merchants there are not more than three or four gentlemen whom we could poffibly recommend to higher ftations at prefent. In this number juftice requires we fhould mention Mr. Campbell, Secretary to this Committee, whofe abilities and indefatigable diligence, of which we had the moft convincing proofs in the courfe of our proceedings, entitle him to this inftance of our regard, and to your particular notice: and as the fame qualifications will diftinguifh him in any ftation of your fervice, it is our joint requeft, that you will pleafe to remove the reftriction on his rifing as a covenant fervant, and fuffer him to take rank according to the date of his appointment. At all times it has been found expedient to deviate occafionally from this general rule of preferring feniority. It now becomes your indifpenfable duty to admit no claim but that of merit, if you would preferve the valuable poffeffions you enjoy, and realize the very near profpect you have of eftablifhing your affairs, on fo firm and folid a bafis as nothing but mifconduct can overfet.

So

So much rests with the Board, that in your judicious, impartial selection of the Members, it depends whether you hold a foot of land, and enjoy a privilege in Bengal; or whether you continue in possession of the most ample revenues and extensive influence ever established by any European mercantile body. We, therefore, most earnestly exhort you, that no consideration of favor, or prejudice be suffered to bias you in the important business of composing your Council; and that no other distinction be admitted, except what is due to ability, to integrity, and to faithful, essential services. Were we to speak our own sentiments further, we would confess it to be our firm opinion, founded on the experience now before us, that the business of this government can never so effectually be conducted as by a select, unanimous Committee. By dividing the power into many hands you weaken authority, promote dissension, and deprive your measures of that secrecy, steadiness, vigour and dispatch necessary to their success. The same means by which you obtained the great advantages you now enjoy, must be continued and

con-

constantly exerted to secure and perpetuate them. And indeed we can think of no other form of government so well adapted, so perfectly consistent to your peculiar present circumstances in Bengal.

31st. It will not be necessary, we apprehend, to dwell upon a refutation of the flimsy, but specious arguments advanced by Mr. Leycester, for immediately filling up the vacancies at the Board, and pursuing the literal sense of your instructions, where you enlarge the Board to sixteen. We have already shewn, and Mr. Leycester does not deny it, that the business of Burdwan and Midnapoor may be conducted to greater advantage by junior servants than by members of the Council. We have also shewn, that enlarging the Council beyond the number required for the business of the presidency and subordinates has proved injurious to the Company. He knows it is our determination, that seven or eight Members should constantly reside at the presidency, while all proper attentions shall be given to your investments and collections; and this we certainly judge to be the spirit of your orders. But if

that

that gentleman means, that no act can be valid that is executed by a less number of Agents than you have expresly appointed, he renders void every deed, covenant, contract and obligation entered into by the Council since the first establishment of this settlement. He even renders null and of no effect, the treaty with the present Nabob, in which he himself had a principal share, and which, we believe, is not signed by more than half the Company's Agents. In a word, we foresee so many inconveniences consequent on a literal compliance with your instructions, that our duty obliges us to suspend, and we think our powers authorize us in suspending at least, if not revoking those orders until your further pleasure be known.

32d. By consulting our proceedings of the 10th of August and 18th September, you will be able to judge of the progress we have made in carrying your orders into execution relative to the trade in salt, beetel-nut and tobacco. This subject we considered with all the attention possible, in regard to your interest and the good of the service. We found, that to remove the inconveniences of a free trade, prevent the oppreſſions daily committed, ſave this valuable article of commerce from ruin, and diffuſe the benefits reſulting indiſcriminately among all your ſervants entitled to duſticks, it was neceſſary to veſt the whole in an excluſive Company; compoſed of the three firſt claſſes of your covenanted ſervants, the field officers, chaplains and head ſurgeons. In admitting the field officers, and ſtating the proportions allotted to each claſs, we had particular regard to the preſent ſituation of your Council and field officers, who are now excluded many emoluments they before enjoyed. It is our opinion, that gentlemen who have riſen to their ſtations with credit and reputation are certainly entitled to ſomething more than a ſubſiſtence. They even have a right to expect ſuch advantages in your ſervice as may enable them to return in a few years, with independence, to their native country. With reſpect to the Company, we are unanimouſly of opinion, it is more for their intereſt to be conſidered as ſuperiors than proprietors: and as the Royal Grant of the Dewannee renders the 11th article unneceſſary, we are there-.

by

by enabled to subject the trade to a duty, which will produce a clear annual revenue of 120,000 pounds sterling. Whatever surplus of their revenues the Company may find themselves possessed of, after discharging all the demands on this presidency, we imagine may be employed much more to their benefit, in supporting and extending the China trade, and assisting the wants of the other presidencies. However, should it either appear, that we have mistaken the Company's real interest, or that the profits of the trade will admit of increased duties, it is our resolution to give all possible satisfaction on these points to our honourable Masters, and to lay before you a fair, full and candid representation of the amount of the costs, charges and sales of the first year.

33d. We think it incumbent on us to observe, that the management of this important business was committed to Mr. Sumner. If the plan, therefore, should prove so fortunate as to meet your approbation, the merit is chiefly due to that gentleman, who spared no pains to acquire a thorough insight into the subject; at the same time that he discharged the duties

duties of the presidency, during Lord Clive's absence, much to our satisfaction. Mr. Sumner would have cheerfully accepted the post of Resident at the Durbar, now grown an employment of consequence, since the grant of the Dewannee: but we judged it to be more becoming his station, more agreeable to your intentions, and more for the benefit of the service, that he should remain at the presidency, to take charge of the government in case of Lord Clive's absence. We, therefore, determine to appoint Mr. Sykes to the Durbar, as he has already sufficiently manifested his capacity and diligence in that employment.

34th. When these dispatches are finished, we resolve to apply ourselves heartily to a reformation of the abuses which have crept into almost all your public offices, and every department, civil and military. The task is arduous, but not impracticable; and we are assured it becomes highly necessary to the service. The same unanimity that has enabled the Committee to dispatch so great a variety of important affairs since their establishment, shall, we hope, be firmly continued and

vigorously

vigoroufly exerted until we have accomplifhed every end propofed at our appointment; until we have ftemmed the torrent of luxury and corruption, and eftablifhed a fpirit of induftry, œconomy and integrity throughout every clafs of your fervants.

35th. We beg leave to conclude with affuring you, that it is the higheft ambition of this Committee to merit the confidence repofed in them, by promoting, with their utmoft diligence and abilities, the honour and intereft of the Eaft-India Company, which have ever been the objects of their moft fervent wifhes.

We have the honour to be, with refpect,

  Honourable Sirs,

    Your moft faithful,

     humble fervants,

(Signed)
{
CLIVE,
WM. B. SUMNER,
JOHN CARNAC,
H. VERELST,
FRAˢ SYKES.
}

Fort William, the 30th September 1765.

SUPPLEMENT.

36th. In juftice to the memory of the late Nabob, Meer Jaffier, we think it incumbent on us to acquaint you, that the horrible maffacres wherewith he is charged by Mr. Holwell, in his addrefs to " The Proprietors of Eaft-India Stock," p. 46. are cruel afperfions on the character of that prince, which have not the leaft foundation in truth. The feveral perfons there affirmed, and who have been generally thought to have been murdered by his order, are all now living, except two, who were put to death by Meeran, without the Nabob's confent or knowledge; and it is with additional fatisfaction we can afsure you, that they were lately releafed from confinement by the prefent Subah; which fully evinces the entire confidence he repofes in the Company's protection againft all attacks on his government.

37th. We are further to acquaint you, that, not fatisfied with paying all due attention to the confirmation and fecurity of your poffeffions in Bengal, Lord Clive has alfo obtained, from the King, Sunnuds for the five northern provinces; and the.

ftrongeft

strongest ratification, under his Majesty's hand and seal, of all your former grants in the Carnatic.

38th. Mr. Sykes has exerted his utmost diligence in procuring an exact estimate of the account of the revenues of the Nabob's dominions; of which *you are now not only the collectors, but the proprietors*; and we were in hopes of transmitting an accurate account of the same by the Admiral Steevens: but the books of the Sircar are so much behind hand, so many balances are outstanding, and such negligence appears in the collection of the revenues for some years past, owing in some measure to the constant disturbances in the country, which prevented any regular collections from being made, that he has not been able yet to succeed to his entire satisfaction; and we therefore think it better to postpone the subject till our next dispatches, when we can write with precision and certainty. At present we can only affirm, that the acquisition of the Dewannee and the agreement with the Nabob will necessarily turn out a prodigious increase of your revenues, and at the same time they must give stability to your power and influence.

39th.

39th. You will observe, in our general letter from the public department, what has passed in Council on the subject of the donation to the navy, which is indeed no more than a transcript of our consultations. We here think it necessary to remark, that we cannot, in the present circumstances of your affairs, and consistently with our late engagements with the Nabob, either take upon us to pay so large a demand out of your revenues, or insist on the Nabob's paying it out of his limited stipend; more especially as it appears that the donation to the navy was never voluntary made, but obtained by force from Meer Jaffier, by dint of solicitations and other means, which never had his entire approbation.

40th. It is with some regret we acquaint you, that we apprehend it will be necessary to resume our late enquiry into the conduct of the gentlemen of the deputation; having just received information from Nundcomar of further sums of money paid to them out of the Nabob's treasury, during their residence at Muxadavad. Mr. Johnstone makes a principal and conspicuous figure in this account

count alfo; having obtained a very large fum, befides what is fpecified in the diftribution lift, or the narratives of Mahomed Reza Cawn and Juggut Seat; which, with the fums received by the other gentlemen, fully accounts for the Nabob's affertions in his letter, addreffed to the Committee. The neceffity we are under of difpatching the fhip, in order to receive the earlieft notice of your fentiments on our proceedings, and your further inftructions, prevents our entering immediately upon the enquiry; of which, however, you may be affured we fhall tranfmit a faithful and particular account in our next advices.

We have the honour to be, with refpect,

Honourable Sirs,

Your moft faithful,

humble fervants,

(Signed,) {
CLIVE,
WM. B. SUMNER,
JOHN CARNAC,
H. VERELST,
FRAs SYKES.
}

Fort William, the 1ft October 1767.

COPY OF A LETTER

FROM

Messrs. RALPH LEYCESTER and GEORGE GRAY,
MEMBERS of the COUNCIL at FORT WILLIAM;

ADDRESSED TO THE

COURT OF DIRECTORS

OF THE EAST-INDIA COMPANY.

Dated the 29th September 1765.

With a Postscript, of the 14th of January 1766.

GENTLEMEN,

THE plan on which your affairs at this Presidency have been conducted, since the arrival of Lord Clive and the other Gentlemen of the Select Committee in Bengal, hath been such as to induce us to make our application to you in a a separate address from the usual channel of correspondence: and we are here to lay before you our sentiments on the conduct of that Committee, from the time they took the supreme and almost entire management of your concerns here into their hands. Our opinion hath differed very widely from theirs in many material points; and no opportunity is allowed us to come to any explanation, far less agreement with them, whilst they persevere in the same tenor of conduct. It is, therefore, become necessary for us to set forth the causes of our difference to you, who alone are the proper judges of the extraordinary powers they have taken into their hands.

Your orders, appointing a Select Committee, are contained in the 67th paragraph of your general letter, of the 1st June 1764, expressed in the following words.

" The General Court of Proprietors, having an account of the critical situation of the Company's affairs in Bengal, requested Lord Clive to take upon him the station of President, and the command of the Company's military forces there. His Lordship has been appointed President and Governor accordingly, as mentioned in the preceding part of this letter. The intention

of

of the General Court in defiring Lord Clive to go to Bengal was, that by his Lordship's character and influence peace and tranquillity might be easier restored and established in that Subaship. In order, therefore, to answer these purposes in a manner that we apprehend may prove most effectual, we have thought proper to appoint a Committee on this occasion; consisting of his Lordship, Mr. William Brightwell Sumner, Brigadier General Carnac, also Messrs. Harry Verelst and Francis Sykes: to whom we do hereby give full powers to pursue whatever means they shall judge most proper to attain those desireable ends. But, however, in all cases where it can be done conveniently, the Council at large is to be consulted by the said Committee, tho' the power of determining is to be in that Committee alone. We further direct, that as soon as peace and tranquillity are restored and established in the Subaship of Bengal, then the said extraordinary powers are immediately to cease, and the said Committee be dissolved.

From the general tenor of your letter, as well as from this particular paragraph, we we think it evident, that the following was the true purport of your orders.

The honourable Company, from the laſt advices they had received from Bengal, conſidered that their affairs at this ſettlement were in a precarious, or even deſperate ſituation.

That Lord Clive having already acquired a great military reputation in India, they eſteemed his Lordſhip a proper perſon to preſide over their Council in that critical juncture, as his character and influence with the country people would give weight to his proceedings.

That as the ſyſtem of military operations requires the utmoſt vigor, expedition and ſecrecy, theſe ends would be better obtained by the management of a Select Committee, than of the whole Council, whoſe number might occaſion a greater difference of opinion, and create more delay in their reſolves.

That they inveſted this Committee with powers to take what ſteps they thought neceſſary for carrying on the war in Bengal, or for putting an end to it; conſulting, however, with the Board on all occaſions where it can be done conſiſtently

with

with the vigor, secrecy and expedition required for the well conducting such transactions. That the powers of this Committee should immediately cease whenever a peace was concluded, and tranquillity restored.

And that all the other branches of the Company's affairs should be carried on by the Council, conformable to the trust reposed in them, on the abolishment of the former Select Committee in your commands of the 9th May 1764; and by the powers of government delegated, by commission, to Lord Clive and fifteen others of the Council.

Such is our idea of the powers you were pleased to confer on the Select Committee; calculated entirely for the dangerous situation of your possessions in Bengal: and we have no reason to doubt that they would have produced the desired effect, had affairs remained in the same precarious state untill Lord Clive and the Committee's arrival, and an occasion had offered that called for an exertion of those qualifications, your opinion of which had induced you to bestow so large a share of the administration on those gentlemen.

But

But very happily for the honourable Company, their affairs had some time before taken a very different turn: and the means with which you had before supplied us, had enabled us, ourselves, to extricate this settlement from the dangers and difficulties with which it had been surrounded: for a particular account of which, we must refer you to our advices by the ships of the last season.

When Lord Clive, therefore, and the other gentlemen of the Committee arrived, they found us on the eve of peace. After a successful war against Shujah Dowlah, they found our army in actual possession of all his country: and although, soon after their arrival, the enemy did make one last struggle for the recovery of their dominions, yet the faintness of their attempt, and the great ease with which they were repelled, shewed it was but like the weak efforts of an expiring blaze. They found the country government of Bengal established on terms highly advantageous for the Company, as well from the great influence they had in the administration, as from the considerable addition of their revenues: and the settlement itself

in

in as flourishing a state as it had known for years past.

Little then to appearance remained, but to dispose of our conquests, and carry into execution the different regulations, civil as well as military, which the honourable Company had pointed out to the Board: and in these we expected no difficulty, as we flattered ourselves, that the cordiality and harmony which subsisted betwixt the Members of the Board, and which we doubted not to meet in those gentlemen, would procure an unanimity in our Councils, and a hearty and uniform co-operation in every measure tending to the interest of our employers.

We are sorry to be undeceived in our hopes, and convinced of the inefficacy of our good intentions: one of the first resolutions formed in their Committee was, that by the Company's orders, in the 67th paragraph of the letter of the first June, already quoted, they were appointed the establishers and guardians of peace, order and tranquillity in these provinces. We must here animadvert, that the word order is an interpolation, which wrests the meaning of that paragraph into a different

different conſtruction from what appears to have been intended. To the military powers you gave, it tended to join the civil juriſdiction: and as if your orders in that paragraph were not a ſufficient baſis on which the extent of the Committee's power could be eſtabliſhed, the defect could only be made up by this expedient.

When the members of the Board, at council, deſired the gentlemen of the Committee to explain the meaning and extent of their powers, the Preſident abſolutely refuſed to come to any explanation on the ſubject with the Board. This jealouſy to have the authority of the Committee canvaſſed, we could not but think carried in itſelf a doubt of its validity; nor could we conſider the terms of the anſwers, but as an earneſt of the little deference or conſideration the Board had to expect from his Lordſhip and the Committee.

Inſtead of the ſatisfaction we had reaſon to expect the Committee would have expreſſed, that the provinces of Bengal were in a ſtate of the moſt perfect tranquillity, and ſettled on terms that not only

only left the Company sole arbiters of the whole country, with a large proportion of its revenues, by the treaty with the Nabob, Najum o' Dowlah, but also so established as to preclude the danger of further revolutions, Lord Clive appeared chagrined and dissatisfied, that we should have taken upon us a step of so much consequence, before the arrival of the Committee, who were particularly charged with those important points; and took frequent opportunities to publish his displeasure at our having prevailed with the Nabob to confirm his agreement with the honourable Company concerning his Jaghire.

We hope the benefits you reap from the treaty with Najum o' Dowlah are too apparent to require an illustration here: but we shall so far obviate his Lordship's reflection as to observe, that we thought the death of the old Nabob, and accession of the new, the properest time to secure the Company's interests: and that as we deemed it more easy to obtain any grants or favours at the beginning of a government, than when possession for a space of time had fixed his title, so it was more eligible than to perplex, or disgust the

the Nabob, by reiterated applications afterwards. Invested with the administration of the Company's affairs, we were authorized to take every measure productive of their good or advantage; and had we neglected that opportunity, to wait for so precarious and uncertain an event as his Lordship's arrival, we should have rendered ourselves deservedly liable to the censure of great inattention to your concerns, or of a conscious incapacity to conduct them.

As to the confirmation of the Jaghire, we think his Lordship makes it a matter of too much consequence. The Company's order to the Board for co-operating with him, proceeded from a supposition he would arrive as soon the order itself. But that not happening to be the case, we secured it for the honourable Company and his Lordship without him; and the acquisition was so very easy, that it was quite immaterial who had the small share of credit which the obtainment of it would acquire. His Lordship needed not to enhance the difficulty, by construing the confirmation into an attempt only; as it must be obvious that the influence

fluence which could prevail for a grant of sixty laaks of rupees *per annum*, could easily obtain the comparatively trifling addition of a reversion of two laaks more.

We have thought it necessary to set forth these circumstances to you, in order to illustrate the spirit and temper of the Committee: and whilst thus determined to assert an authority which, by the tenor of your orders, we could not conceive delegated to them, there could scarce be any prospect of harmony or agreement betwixt them and the Board; whom, accordingly, they treated ever after with slight, and want of consideration, as is very evident from the course of their proceedings.

They called Mr. Verelst from his chiefship at Chittagong, without previously informing the Board, although all appointments had been usually ordered through this channel. This was a needless irregularity, as the Board would never have hesitated to desire that gentleman to leave his factory, in conformity to the honourable Company's commands.

The president having been told, that there was a great balance due from the Burdwan

Burdwan Rajah; and giving implicit credit to this information, without once laying the matter before the Board, or enquiring into the truth of it, or the cause of such deficiency, though it was a branch of the Company's civil affairs, entirely dependent on the public department, assumed the supreme direction, power and management in this matter. A demand was made in consequence on the Rajah, for 790,000 rupees, to be paid in seven days, as the just balance of his revenues, conceived in very absolute terms. His representing the state of the balances, and of the collections and rents outstanding from the farmers, appealing to the public papers for the receipt and application of all the money collected, availed nothing. A peremptory order was sent him to repair to Calcutta, though under the jurisdiction of a Chief and Council, then invested with the whole management, under the immediate orders of the Board, who on this occasion ought certainly to have been consulted. It was scarce possible that the President, or the Committee in so short a time could have been perfectly acquainted with the state of that province, had they even

even previously examined into its accounts, which we believe was not the case. The opinion such a public flight must have raised of the former authority of the Board, and to the prejudice of the Chief of any subordinate in like circumstances, is too apparent to need any comment. The Rajah's conduct shewed the sense he had of it; for after his arrival in Calcutta, and having been kept in suspense for near a fortnight before he was permitted to wait on the President, he durst not pay his compliments to any of the Board, till that very day he was permitted to return to Burdwan.

In so large a collection as that of Burdwan, it is scarce possible but that balances must arise from many casual accidents, which there, as in all other districts, prevent tenants and farmers from paying their rents in full. The Rajah's balance to the Company, notwithstanding the badness of the seasons, and the troubles in the country, was very inconsiderable; and the chief part of it was the balance of the years 1761, and 1762; which might have been cleared off in another year, as the arrears due to the Rajah's

dismissed

dismissed troops was all paid, to a trifle, and a still further reduction might have been made in those kept up. However, after his arrival in Calcutta, he found himself under the necessity of complying, in part, with the demand made upon him: and, not having money in hand, was obliged to borrow from those whom the very high interest of 24 *per cent.* would induce to lend him. A payment thus obtained, is no better than a transfer of the debt from the Company to private merchants, with the additional incumbrance of an interest, amounting to near a quarter of the original demand: and which, if ever paid, must come out of the Burdwan treasury. The rigorous exertion of such an authority over even debtors to the Company, when the same end can be obtained by more moderate measures, can serve, we think, no good purpose. The Governor of this presidency, receiving the approbation of the Council, may, we allow, at any time examine into the management of every branch of your affairs: but we cannot admit of his holding any powers of this kind independent of them. We do not
mean,

mean, or wish to derogate from the authority of the Governor; but to affert, that, confiftent with the terms of your commiffion, he can have no right to the authority he exercifed, but in conjunction with his Council: nor, in the prefent cafe, could there be the fmalleft plea for not afking their concurrence; for the intereft and credit of the Council muft ever be concerned to fupport the Governor in the exercife of all due authority.

To the fame effect was Mr. Verelft's appointment to Burdwan: who, though the Company's intereft in that province had been managed for years paft to the entire fatisfaction of the Board as well as of the Court of Directors, being a member of the Select Committee, is nominated Supervifor from the Committee: and having received his appointment from thofe gentlemen, is in a manner independent of, and fuperior to the orders of Council: which appears to us to be a total breach of the rules by which your fervice has been conducted, and feems to caft an odium on the former Prefidents and their Councils, or to reflect on their integrity,

integrity, ability, or attention to direct those affairs.

The young Nabob, Najum o' Dowlah, had, on his acceffion to the Subahdarry, followed the cuftom of his predeceffors, in beftowing prefents on the gentlemen in ftation; who, having eftablifhed the Company's interefts on the moft beneficial terms, thought themfelves at liberty, without incurring cenfure, to accept what had been given by former Nabobs in a far greater proportion. The Nabob happened, at the fame time, to have a perfonal diflike to Mahomed Reza Cawn, who was appointed Naib Subah by the Board contrary to his inclination. When the Nabob came to Calcutta, to vifit his Lordfhip, he complained againft Mahomed Reza Cawn: and as an argument to induce his Lordfhip to difplace Mahomed Reza Cawn from a fhare of the government, he fet forth, that the treaty was not according to his inclination, but forced upon him; and that Mahomed Reza Cawn had embezzled twenty laaks of rupees, in diftributions amongft the gentlemen, without his confent. It is evident, in this complaint, the Nabob

was

was actuated by no other motive but his desire of dismissing Mahomed Reza Cawn from the appointment the Council had conferred upon him: and he imagined, that the extraordinary favours his deceased father had heaped on Lord Clive had confirmed him a steady friend to his family; and, therefore, that, on the first complaint against Mahomed Reza Cawn, his Lordship would not hesitate at his removal. In this vain notion he was encouraged by several who disliked Mahomed Reza Cawn's promotion, but particularly by Nundcomar, who, though at professed variance with the principal gentlemen of the deputation, was in fact the person who chiefly advised the Nabob to make presents, and was greatly interested in Mahomed Reza Cawn's removal.

It was, therefore, the dislike to Mahomed Reza Cawn which occasioned the complaint. But Lord Clive, setting entirely aside the Nabob's inclination, made that the principal object of his enquiry, which was only designed as an inducive, although unjust argument. The presents were immediately canvassed: Mahomed

Reza Cawn came down from the city, was called upon, and (in his narrative to the Committee of the 6th June) cleared himself of the charge of having difpofed of the Nabob's money without his confent, by producing orders under the Nabob's own hand and feal for its payment. We muft take notice, that Mahomed Reza Cawn was for fome time kept in great fufpenfe by the Committee, whether he was to be continued in his appointment of Naib Subah, or not; and fuch apparent encouragement was given to the perfon who might be deemed his rival, that it is not to be wondered he fhould purfue the meafures which appeared to him moft fuitable to fecure his promotion with Lord Clive, who was become the arbiter of his title to it; and, with this view, he related what appears in his narratives to the Committee. We would not infer, that the Committee kept Mahomed Reza Cawn in this fupenfe with any fuch view: yet it is our opinion he could not but be influenced, by fuch his fituation, to afperfe a fet of gentlemen to whom he was under the higheft obligations. From the pains taken before to intimate through the whole

whole country, that the business of importance was taken by the Company out of the hands of the gentlemen of the former Council, and lodged in those of the Select Committee alone, the officers of the government would doubtless look on its Members as the objects of their courtship; and from particular intimations, as we understand, given Mahomed Reza Cawn, Roydullub and others, on their arrival in Calcutta, not to visit, or have any intercourse with the gentlemen of Council, the light in which these were in future to be considered was very obviously pointed out.

Every one, whom a long residence in India hath made conversant with the manners and principles of its inhabitants, must know, from frequent experience, how much they are influenced in their conduct by their hopes, or their fears, when they themselves are interested. Truth hath not with them its force, but is always rendered subservient to their private interests. A temporary accommodation to their circumstances is the sole view in their assertions, professions, declarations. They cannot, from their own notions, distinguish

tinguish betwixt a defire of obtaining real information, and that of encouraging the moft injurious criminations. Strangers to the candor of our laws, and folely guided by the maxims of their own arbitrary government, they confider a ftrict enquiry as a fixed defign to ruin. Betwixt the hopes of obtaining a government then, and the apprehenfions of lofing it, we think it will not appear extraordinary, that Mahomed Reza Cawn fhould give whatever informations he thought might prove injurious to the gentlemen of the former adminiftration, whom he had the greateft reafon, as well from the prevalent reports as from the nature of the enquiries, to believe were held on ill terms by thofe now in power.

But what more particularly invalidates the evidence of Mahomed Reza Cawn, the accufer was never once confronted with the accufed, that the latter might have an opportunity to confute him perfonally: nor was it ever known that he was examined till the Committee were pleafed to inform the Board of it, for the enquiry was made with the greateft fecrecy; fo that we have nothing of our own knowledge

ledge to depend on. It is however evident, that Mahomed Reza Cawn was required to lodge all the information he could: for besides clearing himself from the Nabob's charge, which was all that was necessary for him, and was done by producing orders under the Nabob's hand for all he had expended, in his second declaration, of the 6th June, he discovers his private offers; not only to the deputation, but also his presents to the former President, months before the old Nabob's death, though only an usual compliment on his accession to the chair: a most invidious and unbecoming task. Had Mahomed Reza Cawn informed the Committee of what he offered, and was not accepted, as well as what was, they would have known, that he tendered Mr. Gray a considerable present which he chose to refuse: and that gentleman declares his opinion, that as Mahomed Reza Cawn was so forward in offering his services to him without solicitation, there is no reason to think but that the presents to the other gentlemen came also unsolicited.

As things are situated, no dependence can be placed on the testimony of such a

biassed

biassed witness. And we think it worthy of remark, that though Lord Clive, when he first came, seemed to disapprove of such an officer as a Naib Subah, and although Mahomed Reza Cawn had been so very instrumental in the practices so highly arraigned, yet Lord Clive has thought fit to continue the government in his hands.

Juggut Seat's narrative was evidently, according to his own declaration, demanded from him. But what we are going to relate of the evidence brought to support his charge must, we think, shock the ear of every man who claims the liberty derived from our constitution. Mooteram, formerly a servant of Mr. Johnstone, was seized in his house, by guards: and after being closely confined, by Lord Clive, under all the horrors of an armed force, is carried before the Committee, there, with the terrors a man must feel under such circumstances, to answer whatever interrogatories they thought proper to put to him. Various questions were proposed to the trembling prisoner, to his own and his master's prejudice. This was transacted in the Committee:

and

and their comments were fixed to what he said; though we must do the civil Members of the Committee the justice to remark, that it does not appear, from their proceedings, that the military guards were placed over Mooteram by any authority of theirs, but by Lord Clive's, singly.] We could not fail to be alarmed at such an extraordinary proceeding; since, under such circumstances, neither the character nor properties of your servants, who may be thought at variance with Lord Clive, are secure: for what man will dare to bear testimony in our favor, when he is either overawed by the dread of such violence and resentment, or thinks it his interest to with-hold the evidence that would acquit us?

On the illegality of these proceedings being pointed out at the Board, Lord Clive proposed to have at least one examination conducted at the Board: and Mooteram, with his guards, being called before them, the same questions which had been asked him in the Committee, with his answer, to which he had been bound down by oath, were read and interpreted to him: and he was asked, if they

they were true, or not. As Mooteram had before been sworn at the Committee, he could not, without being guilty of perjury, have denied his former evidence. It was, therefore, quite unneceſſary to have him re-examined. We are to remark, that though Mooteram complained of the hardſhip he ſuffered, from being under a guard, it was not till after repeated intreaties, and after all his depoſitions were finiſhed, that Lord Clive ſet him at liberty.

We muſt obſerve, that we do not intend to exculpate Mr. Johnſtone's conduct, that gentleman has to anſwer for himſelf: we only mean to illuſtrate the meaſures purſued in the courſe of their enquiries.

The proceedings of the Committee have been ſometimes, on the ſubject of their ſcrutiny, read to the Board: but Lord Clive did not think proper to permit their being entered in our conſultation. Why they ſhould be kept ſo myſterious a ſecret we know not, ſince matters of ſuch moment as charges againſt Members of the Board, ought to be examined and recorded in the moſt public manner. But the Committee have on this occaſion formed them-

themselves into a Court of Enquiry, and, with the Minutes of Council laid before them, have passed their judgments on our conduct, as if they were superior to the Council: a supposition we deem as incongruous as, that a part can be greater than the whole: for the powers of the Council are delegated unto them by a formal commission, authorizing the President and fifteen other Members to conduct the whole of the Company's affairs within the jurisdiction of this settlement. Whereas those of the Committee are no more than particular instructions, transmitted in the general letters through the channel of the Board: and are only relative, as we have before observed, to the military branch of government, and such transactions as require secrecy.

With this opinion of their own superior authority, the Select Committee were pleased to adjudge the Members of Council guilty of a breach of your orders, in their omission to execute the covenants sent out *per* Lapwing; thinking themselves extremely moderate, in being satisfied with only passing this censure on us. But as we have hitherto made a strict attention to your interests, and obedience to your orders, the rules of our conduct, we cannot divest ourselves of the hope, that you will not consider us as deficient in duty to you on this occasion.

Your orders touching the covenants seemed to us not so peremptory, as to exclude us from expostulating with you on the occasion: our execution of them was of no particular moment to the Company, but was a hardship on their servants, by laying us under a restraint unknown to our predecessors in your service. We are well apprized the resolution of binding down your servants by such an obligation was the result of contests at home, and seemed particularly derived from the dispute concerning Lord Clive's jaghire; and you yourselves inform us it was the determination of a General Court of Proprietors, by ballot. We have seen instances of orders enforced in stronger terms than those concerning the covenants repealed on a proper representation: and we were not without the hopes of prevailing with you on the present occasion to reverse them; nay, perhaps a subsequent Court of Proprietors might of them-

themselves alter them. It was for this reason that the covenants were not immediately executed when they were received, but deferred till Lord Clive's arrival, to come under confideration with the other regulations directed in your letter of the 1st June 1764, when we expected to be better informed of your final resolves; and in the mean time it had been determined to address you on the subject by the latter ship: but on the Bute's dispatch, the attention of the Board having been engaged in confiderations more material to your interests on the late Nabob's death, the covenants, we confess, escaping the Board's recollection, were entirely overlooked; else how easy would it have been for us to have represented, by that conveyance, the arguments we have set forth to the Board since, and now lay before you.

When the covenants arrived, we had no immediate prospect of benefiting by a delay in their execution; for the old Nabob was living, and what happened after could never have been pre-imagined: and had the Board but taken the precaution then of resolving, on the face of their

con-

consultation, to refer that part of your commands back to the honourable Company, and to wait for their further orders, the Committee would not have been furnished with any pretence now to call them to account. This was a very obvious step, and the omission shewed we entertained no other intention than that of only waiting till the arrival of the expected Members of the Board from Europe. This we hope will suffice to convince you we intended no breach of your orders by the delay. Your commands for laying open the inland trade, by granting dustucks to the free merchants, which tended to the disadvantage of your servants, were more peremptory; but the suspension of that order, when the arguments of the Board were heard, was approved of, and the order itself reversed.

The covenants do not seem so much to forbid our receiving presents, as they oblige us to acquaint the Company of what are made us, and to stand to their determination as to their disposal. What we accepted, therefore, would have been no breach of the covenants, even had we executed them before the acceptance, and

we

we should not have scrupled to have submitted the presents to the conditions of the covenant, had not the Committee made that violent attack upon us, and by the severity of their measures totally destroyed the merit of such a voluntary submission.

Some gentlemen of the Council, in their answers to the charge against them, objected to the authority of the Select Committee in a research of this nature: and to these Lord Clive and the Members of the Committee replied in minutes, on the face of the consultations on the 20th of June. His Lordship's minute, although more particularly relative to Mr. Johnstone, yet affects the rest of the Council who happened to concur in opinion with him concerning the Committee's stretch of power. His Lordship observes, it is not incumbent on him to vindicate the powers with which the Committee is invested: we never demanded any vindication of them, for we never arraigned the powers granted by the Company to the Committee. We think they are fully pointed out in the general letter, quoted in the former part of this address; and, as commands from

from our superiors, we pay the utmost obedience to them: but it is the extending of these powers beyond the meaning of your orders which requires to be vindicated.

The honourable Company have deemed the authority of the Board of such moment, that they have been pleased to grant a Special Commission, empowering a President and fifteen other Members of Council to transact all their affairs. Had they appointed the Select Committee superior to the Council, it is most probable that they would have delegated such extraordinary powers in the ampleſt form, as they abſolutely did, in a ſeparate letter of the 8th February 1763, to Mr. Vanſittart, or in his abſence, to his ſucceſſor and a Select Committee; which by marking out their extent, would at once have put them out of doubt: but hitherto we have ſeen no ſuch powers, nor do we believe they exiſt. We, therefore, cannot but eſteem the only commiſſion of adminiſtration to be the ſupreme one, and conſider every infringement of that as a violation of the authority which conferred it: and we ſhould be unworthy of the truſt repoſed

posed in us, by our superiors, if we suffered any such to pass unnoticed, or unopposed.

But in defect of any deed of special powers from the Company to the Committee, his Lordship has been pleased to give the Board a narrative of his motives and inducements for coming to India, as an explanation of the Company's orders of the 1st June. His Lordship will excuse us if we cannot admit a private representation to have, in any respect, the weight of an order from the Company, or if we should not be biassed to admit of constructions contrary to their evident sense and meaning.

We are very willing to ascribe to his Lordship all the merit due to his distinguished character; and we do, without scruple, suppose his views in taking charge of this government were perfectly disinterested, as to advantages of fortune; but we do not grant that the affairs of this Presidency were in such a desperate situation as to require his aid to save the settlement from inevitable ruin. Some irregularities and abuses there might have been in both the civil
and

and military branches of the service, such as will require the constant attention of the Board to correct and regulate; nor can his Lordship say, that when he quitted the government of Bengal, in the year 1760, he left it in such a state as not to be liable to the same imputation, and to require an equal share of improvement. The constant state of warfare we have been engaged in for years past engrossed much of the Board's attention, nor were the circumstances of our affairs, or temper of our army, well adapted to reformation. The Board considered the regulations, contained in your letter of the 1st June, as directed more particularly to Lord Clive and the other Members of the Board in conjunction with him, and therefore deferred those changes till his Lordship's arrival. However, considering that the greater the danger and difficulties seem to be, the more honour would be acquired in the extrication, we are not surprized that Lord Clive should take pains to set forth to the world a notion of the settlement's impending ruin.

We

We cannot help taking notice of his Lordship's want of civility to the Council, when he tells them, they were officious in procuring the confirmation of the terms he had agreed on with the Company respecting his jaghire. Such an unbecoming censure might have been spared the Board, as well as the invidious motives he ascribes for that step. We declare the Board had no other view but that, as they were forming a treaty with the Nabob, a provisionary clause should be reserved for that agreement.

The minute delivered in by the other Members of the Select Committee seems to insinuate, that they had met with an opposition from the Board to measures that were for the Company's interests and advantage; as if the other Members of the Board were not devoted to the Company, and had their welfare at heart equally with themselves. We are truly concerned to see an allegation made use of that seems calculated to acquire the Committee a credit with the Company at the expence of gentlemen who by no means deserved such a reflection. We defy the Committee to point out a single salutary regulation to which

which we have ever objected, or to any regulations whatever at the time that minute was delivered in. Indeed they have put our opinions of any measures they had to propose out of the question, for they have assumed from the Board what the Company expressly entrusted to the management of Council; and it is to this stretch of power and authority alone that any objections have ever been made.

Complaints against the sudden growth of wealth is, we think, a very extraordinary argument out of the mouth of the Committee: for in the midst of immense fortunes suddenly acquired, Lord Clive's stands the most conspicuous. However, as the honourable Company have not intimated any such severity to their servants, as the desire of depriving them of a competency honestly procured, so if the Company are displeased with the affluence of their servants, it must be when unjustly got, or when it is employed to their prejudice, or disadvantage.

When Lord Clive had finished his eager enquiries touching the presents, they applied themselves to regulate the offices of the Nabob's government; but without
consulting

consulting the Board, or even informing them of a single determination they had come to, or any plan they had settled; and to this time we are kept in ignorance of the particulars of that transaction, except in what we have heard by common report: which leaves us room to remark, that while most of the settlement are acquainted with the resolutions of the Committee on this subject, the Council are to this day uninformed of them.

After these points were adjusted, the Nabob left Calcutta; but without receiving the usual ceremony of a visit of leave from the Board at his departure, which had never before been omitted. As to Mahomed Reza Cawn and Doolubram, they strictly adhered to what they conceived to be the intent of the Committee, that they should keep up no intercourse with the Members of Council during their stay in Calcutta. Visits are so usual and necessary a mark of civility in Hindostan, that their omission is reckoned the greatest disrespect: and without an intimation, it is impossible that those very men, who had before been on a footing of great intimacy and correspondence with us,

would

would have dared to be guilty of the neglect; conscious themselves of the incivility, some of these officers made a private apology for their behaviour, declaring their inclination to cultivate terms of friendship with us, but that they durst not, through fear of incurring his Lordship's displeasure.

When the Ministers of the Nabob's government are so closely connected with ours, they must be anxiously concerned in every change which happens amongst us. Such an estrangement from the Council can have no other tendency than to point out they are, in future, to esteem both Lord Clive and themselves, as it were, at variance with us; and under this notion they have been allowed to be wanting in the respect due to our rank and station in your service, as if Lord Clive's authority in the points committed to his charge could not be sufficiently displayed if the least shadow remained to the Board. How injurious it is to the Council, and how detrimental to your affairs, thus to have the influence of the Board degraded in the eyes of a country to be managed under their direction, we

leave

leave it to you to judge; but surely, whatever moderation the Council may preserve from motives prudential for your interests, they cannot but be extremely disgusted under such circumstances.

These points being settled, Lord Clive now prepares to proceed towards Ilihabad, to negotiate with the King and Sujah ul Dowla. As the Committee had extended their authority, and infringed on the province of the Council in other cases, which the Company, in our opinion, entrusted to the administration of the Board, it was not to have been expected, that in their own particular sphere they would yield such a concession to the Board, as to communicate their sentiments or intentions on the subject of his Lordship's Commission, although the Company direct, that the Board should be consulted where they conveniently can; yet this being left to the Committee's discretion, they may be supposed the best judges of the convenience: we, therefore, did not deem ourselves absolutely entitled to be consulted, nor expressed any dissatisfaction that such a compliment was not paid to the Board; nor did we ever attempt to make this, nor any

any matter which, by your commands, comes under the department of the Select Committee, a subject of debate. Without any intimation then of their sentiments relative to this point, his Lordship took his leave of the Board, informing them he was going up the country on affairs of importance.

Soon after his Lordship's departure, the Committee informed the Board, that there was some particular business to be transacted at the Durbar, which required the presence of Mr. Sykes, and that he was about to proceed to the city. As Mr. Middleton was Resident already at the Durbar, and it was his province to transact all the business there, the Board were surprized at such a motion, considering it was an unjust reflection on a gentleman who had all along conducted himself to their entire satisfaction; and they proposed, that the present business should be entrusted to Mr. Middleton, as all these matters had been heretofore. This the Committee refused: alledging it required great secrecy, and ought not to be communicated but to one of their own members. They assured the Board, however,

ever, that the appointment of Mr. Sykes should not injure Mr. Middleton's authority, who was to be independent of him, and to remain representative on the part of the Council.

As in Lord Clive's former government in Bengal, and for a long time afterwards, the residence to the Durbar had been given to servants below the rank of Council, yet no scruple was ever made to entrust them with the most material and secret transaction relative to the government; and as the Committee are obliged to employ a secretary and assistants in the course of their business, we could see no reason why Mr. Middleton, bound by an oath of secrecy, was not fully as worthy of confidence and trust as these gentlemen, had it been even a matter of the strictest secrecy. But as the Committee had before acquainted the Board, that Mahomed Reza Cawn's timidity in the administration had given Roydullub too much sway, which must be checked, and that to effect this was the business which required Mr. Sykes to proceed to Moorshedabad; after such intimation given to the Board, where was the necessity of keeping it concealed from Mr. Middleton, one of its members, who could fully as well accomplish this end as Mr. Sykes? Or what occasion was there to keep two of the Council at the Durbar, when one only was sufficient for all the business, and the other would remain an instance, to the whole country, how cheaply the Council were rated by the Committee? whilst, at the same time, a separate and divided interest between them was thus publicly pointed out.

But we learn by a letter from Mr. Middleton to the Board, that the appointment to the Durbar was intended Mr. Sykes all along, and before he left Calcutta: disgusted, therefore, with his situation, he resigned this appointment, and claimed the vacant Chiefship of Patna: which having been designedly left open, by desire of the Committee, to provide for some such occasion, was allotted him.

When Mr. Sykes was at the city, Lord Clive being on his way to Illihabad, General Carnac at the head of the army, and Mr. Verelst at Burdwan, of the whole Committee, only Mr. Sumner remained at Calcutta, a single member. He not of himself

himself forming a Committee, there was a total suspension of the regular administration of the Company's affairs. The Committee esteeming themselves the supreme power, had appointed their own members to different stations: who being dispersed, and not acknowledging the authority of the Council, each acted in his own station, independent of the orders of the Board, and absolutely without controul: and as none but the Committee have the power to assemble its members together, so the date of their separate independent authority rested with themselves entirely. We need here only remark, that this is a form of government altogether new, and unknown in this settlement before.

During this state of interregnum, it had been proposed in Council to fill up two seats rendered vacant, by the death of Mr. Billers and Mr. Johnstone's resignation, that the number which the Company had directed to the management of their affairs, by their Commission of government and in their letter of the 1st June, might be complete. To this proposal it was objected, on the part of the Committee,

mittee, and the Board were informed, that they were about to make regulations for reducing the number of Council: it was, therefore, defired that we would defer coming to a refolution on the prefent motion for nominating new members. We muft own we were no lefs alarmed than furprized to hear a meafure propofed which, in our opinion, was not only an open violation of the Company's immediate and moft pofitive order, but alfo an invafion of their authority and prerogative. Our employers had iffued a Commiffion, under the great feal of the the Company, appointing a Prefident and fifteen other members to the management of all their concerns in Bengal; and in their accompanying letter had, in as full and ample terms as poffible, ordered, that whenever any vacancies fhould happen in that number, fuch vacancies fhould be filled up by the next of their fervants in feniority, provided no objections were made to their character. This commiffion doth as abfolutely empower and authorize the loweft member of the fixteen, nominally appointed by the Company, or of their fucceffors, to be agent for the Company,

pany, as it doth the President himself; and to dispute or invalidate this authority, or right of agency in the youngest of the sixteen members, is, in our opinion, to dispute or invalidate the commission itself. Such an infringement of the commission is absolutely superseding its authority: and after the validity of the commission is thus set aside, the power of government exercised is not what the Company delegated, but an assumed and usurped one. To act from any other authority but that which the Company have conferred is admitting, that another body hath a right to direct and prescribe in such case equal with, or superior to the Company; which supposition we consider as a direct breach of their orders, and an infringement of their authority and prerogative, in a point that most nearly affects their very constitution.

It is not for us to prescribe what form of government we imagine to be the best: the Company have the undoubted right to dictate to us the system most agreeable to them, and it is our duty implicitly to be guided by their orders in so nice a point. While we hold our power according

cording to the laws prescribed us, should any casual inconveniences or miscarriages arise, they must fall upon our employers; but if once, throwing aside the form established by the Company, we erect systems of our own, from that moment we become accountable and responsible for every bad consequence that may immediately, or in future, accrue. If we have any alterations in the systems of government to propose, which we may deem improvements, and for the benefit of our employers, it would be consistent with our duty to set them forth to the Company, and to wait their approbation before such alterations are carried into execution.

It also occurred to us, that the two next gentlemen in the succession were by the Company's appointment absolutely entitled to a share of the administration: to exclude them, therefore, was an act of injustice, and privation of their right. It would be just as absurd to suppose, that the second in Council could be set aside from his succession to the government in case of vacancy, if there should be a majority disposed to deprive him of this

this appointment, as those gentlemen from their seats at the Board.

Influenced by these considerations and sentiments, we could not consent to a measure we thought inconsistent with our duty to you, and our own judgments: and upon a division of voices, the majority were of opinion, that the number of Council should be completed. Mr. Charlton and Mr. French, the two gentlemen next to Council, were thereupon appointed to fill up the vacancies, and directed to repair to the Presidency, and take their seats at the Board, as soon as convenient.

Your directions concerning the inland trade, in the articles of salt, beetel-nut and tobacco, seemed to be a matter merely commercial, and particularly addressed to the management of the Council: yet Lord Clive and the Committee have taken upon themselves to form such regulations as they have thought proper, without the concurrence, or even asking the opinion of the Board. Although we had reason to be dissatisfied, that no attention was paid to our opinion, though we considered ourselves entitled to be consulted, yet,

yet, knowing the Committee were determined to carry their fyftem into execution, we contented ourfelves with only entering a diffent: but at the fame time cheerfully contributed our fervices, when, by the direction of the Board, we were appointed members of a committee of trade, for executing the plan formed by the Select Committee.

Relative to this trade, the recallment of European agents is another inftance where the Committee have taken upon themfelves to conduct what belonged to the province of the Board; which was fo much the more unneceffary, as the Prefident and Council had before teftified their readinefs to comply with the Company's inftructions on this head, by iffuing orders to the fame effect.

Lord Clive, having returned to the prefidency, laid before the Board the articles of a treaty he had concluded with the King and Shujah Dowlah together, with the Sunnuds obtained, from the King, for the Dewannee and perpetual Jaghire of the royal revenues of Bengal, Bahar and Orixa: with Sunnuds of confirmation for the counties of Burdwan, Midnapoor

Midnapoor and Chittagong, before held by the Company.

With refpect to the treaty with Shujah Dowlah, the former Board had, at different times, endeavoured to effect a peace with that prince, on fuch conditions as were deemed proper and honourable: but whilft he had any forces to oppofe us, he rejected all our offers; and rather than confent to our terms, he preferred an attempt to form a confederacy with all the powers he could ftir up againft us; partly by the pretext of a holy war, wherein he invited the different princes of the Mahomedan faith to oppofe our ambitious views of conqueft, and partly by offers of money. Finding our propofals fruitlefs, and the King coming over to us, after the important victory of Buxar, to which alone we are indebted for the prefent tranquillity and happy ftate of the Company's affairs, the Board entered into negotiations with his Majefty.

We engaged to put the King in poffeffion of Shujah Dowlah's dominions: and he, in return, made over to the Company, by his Sunnuds, the perpetuity of the province of Gauzepore, with all Bul-

U wantfing's

wantsing's Zemindarry, as an indemnification for their losses; and promised farther, to defray the expences of the war from the time our troops were employed in his service. We had also engaged, with the King's concurrence, our promise of the Subahdarry of Illihabad to Najeef Khan; a brave and active prince, who had heartily joined our interests, and on whom, as well on account of a family quarrel with Shujah Dowlah as for other reasons, we could perfectly depend: we had actually put him in possession of it; and had further intended to have procured from the King his appointment to the Subahdarry of Oud.

It was our desire of adhering to these our engagements, which latterly precluded all terms of peace with Shujah Dowlah; who, though haughty and stubborn whilst he could raise a single Rohilla or Maratta to support his cause, yet being deprived of every inch of territory, his treasure exhausted, deserted by almost all his people, reduced to the state of as mere an exile and wanderer as Mhir Cossim himself, and forced to take shelter with Ahmud Khan Bengush,

Bengufh, who afforded him nothing more than the protection of hofpitality, he was at laſt forced to make humble ſuit to his victors, and was ſure to rejoice in any terms, when not a ſingle grant was in his hands to cede to us. But the Board conſidered, that to reſtore Shujah Dowlah to his dominions, would have been an infringement of their treaty with the King; which was now ſo much the leſs neceſſary for the tranquillity of the country, as the King was in actual poſſeſſion of them.

The Board conſidered themſelves as no longer acting in any other capacity but as allies to the King: and thinking the war in a manner at an end, ordered the Commander in Chief to acquaint the King, now that we had put him in poſſeſſion of the provinces of Oud and Illihabad, we conſidered our part of the engagements towards him as fulfilled, and that it was not our intention to carry on ſo expenſive a war, at ſuch a diſtance from our own diſtricts, any longer; but that he muſt take his meaſures to ſupport himſelf in the poſſeſſions we had acquired for him, by acting with his utmoſt vigour. Our view herein was to ſtimulate the

King and Najecf Khan to exert themſelves in their own cauſe, as well as to convince ourſelves how far the King could actually effect what he had before confidently aſſured us of, the maintaining himſelf with his own ſtrength, whenever a conqueſt was made of Shujah Dowlah's country. For he had given us the ſtrongeſt aſſurances, that whenever we ſhould put him in poſſeſſion of the provinces of Oud and Illihabad, many country powers, devoted to him in their hearts, would flock to his ſtandard, and that he would then be enabled to recover Delhi, the ſeat of his empire. The ſureſt way to come to a certainty how far he could maintain himſelf on the ſupport of his own ſtrength, was to convince him of the neceſſity of his exertion; for as long as he had a proſpect of our army fighting his battles, ſolely relying on his aſſiſtance, he would take no ſtep whatever in ſupport of his own cauſe; nor would he even take the neceſſary care and concern of his government.

The treaty now entered upon has created a total change in the King's affairs: ſo near as he was to power and independence,

dependence, he had never felt himself before master of Shujah Dowlah. He is restored to his former dominions, and to the Vizarut: and has stipulated to pay the Company fifty laaks in thirteen months, as well by way of indemnification for damages sustained in the war, as for the surrender of your territories of Gauzepore, &c. of which the revenues for the next year are assigned over for payment of twenty laaks, in part of the above stipulated sum.

As to the Royal Sunnuds for the lands of Burdwan, Midnapore and Chittagong, the King having in fact no real power in Bengal, we were extremely cautious in admitting his authority over the disposal of its lands or revenues. His Majesty had bestowed several Sunnuds for jaghires in the Bengal provinces on his adherents and favourites, to a very considerable yearly amount; one particularly to Major Munro, for a large yearly income, which that gentleman honourably gave up into the hands of the late Nabob. Did we openly acknowledge the King's prerogative to grant Sunnuds by an application for those, we could not with decency have

have denied the validity of thefe: and a large revenue would have been drained from the provinces for the ufe of feveral officers of the King's Court, which we did not think prudent to allow of.

The Board had it certainly in their power to obtain the above-mentioned Sunnuds from the King, as well as thofe for the Dewannee, and perpetual jaghirat of Bengal, Bahar and Orixa, had they thought it for your intereft and advantage: for the King, hitherto fupported by our treafure and arms, and in a ftate of abfolute dependence on our government, had it fcarce in his power to refufe complying with any requefts we fhould make: and fuch a grant, far from being at his own expence or privation, would rather prove beneficial to him, by fecuring us as guarantees for a certain revenue from Bengal, from which we believe for fome years paft he has drawn very little advantage. It is not to be doubted then, but that the King would have beftowed upon us a grant for the poffeffion of a country where he had not the leaft power, but through our influence, as eafily before, as he had done now: but motives, which

which we deemed the moſt weighty and material, forbad our making an application for ſuch a grant.

The Board had conſidered the benefits received by the Company from Mhir Jaffier, and the nature of the connections which ſubſiſted with him, as ſufficient reaſons to enter into engagements with his eldeſt ſon, Najum o' Dowlah, with whom accordingly a treaty was ratified, as ſolemn as the pledge of our public faith and promiſe could make it, and on terms which ſeemed to us beneficial: and we refer it to our employers, whether they were ſo or not. We thought we could not, without a violation of this treaty and of our public faith, as well as of the ties of gratitude, accept of favours, or demand powers from the King that were ſo incompatible with our engagements with the Nabob, and detrimental to a family from whom ſuch ample benefits had been derived. Beſides, although the Dewannee was, we know, an acquiſition equal to a Sovereignty in point of power, and that it would yield ſome increaſe of revenue; yet, as the honourable Company informed us they were ſatisfied with their preſent

sent possessions, and by no means desirous of extending them, we apprehended, that to appropriate to themselves the revenues and command of a kingdom was greatly exceeding their desires and intentions, and though bringing them a present temporary advantage, yet, in the end, might be attended with consequences in the highest degree prejudicial to their true interests: and we did not doubt but they had the prudential consideration in view, when they set the limits they did to our acquisitions; and that they will be fully satisfied with the large additional income stipulated for them, by our treaty with Najum o' Dowlah, before Lord Clive arrived.

Such were the motives of the former administration, and such our objections to pursuing the measures which have been lately adopted. However, since the gentlemen of the Committee have been able to surmount the scruples we entertained, it might, in a political view, be esteemed a happy circumstance that gives the finishing hand to a peace after we had brought the war so near a conclusion, did it, at the same time, put an end to such distant

distant connections as those with his Majesty. But we must observe, that as we are guarantees in the treaty made by Lord Clive, we must support the King in possession of the small district allotted him: and being in offensive and defensive alliance with Shujah Dowlah, we are under the necessity of assisting him whenever he shall be attacked by the different powers of Hindostan. Under such circumstances, our present situation may possibly not be found better than had the Board's agreement with the King been adhered to: and in the latter case, the English would have avoided the imputation of violating their engagements, and of adopting new and contrary systems on every change of their own government; which we think must tend to destroy the confidence heretofore placed in their promises, treaties and alliances. But to admit, for a moment, the expediency and propriety of his Lordship's system of putting an end to the war, still we think the settlement for the King very injudiciously made: he is seated in as remote a country as he well could be, at the utmost extent of Shujah Dowlah's dominions, and in that territory

X we

we have engaged to maintain him. Should then the King happen to be attacked, a body of our troops are to march an immense way from our own provinces, before they arrive to yield the King assistance. We know the King is like to have no support but in us; all the territory, therefore, assigned him may be lost before our troops could join him: and as Shujah Dowlah, whose fidelity and engagements are very doubtful, will be between our own districts and those we are to protect, the division of our forces, unavoidable in case the King should be attacked, will afford him the finest opportunity to vindicate his injured reputation and gratify his resentment to the English, and to recover the district allotted to the King. All these evils might have been avoided, we think, by placing the King in the Zemindarry of Bulwantsing; who would with more pleasure have paid his revenues to the King than he now does to Shujah Dowlah. Bulwantsing's Zemindarry being immediately on our own borders, we could with less difficulty and danger have guaranteed the King in possession of it. Bulwantsing would have been benefited by such a

settlement,

settlement, and happy in the security and protection his Zemindarry must have received from us. In case of a future war with Shujah Dowlah, he would have afforded us some assistance; and by his admitting us to garrison the two fortresses of Juanpore and Chinar-Gurr, we should have possessed the strongest and most natural barriers and bulwarks to our own provinces, and the direct inroad to Shujah Dowlah's dominions, which might have kept him awe. How a Settlement so obviously calculated to secure ourselves from future attacks from that quarter, and to insure a revenue to the King, happened to escape his Lordship, we are at a loss to account for: we deem it evident he has been greatly mistaken in his politicks.

As the Committee have also reconciled to the Company's interests the addition of an income which may arise by the Dewannee, we freely ascribe to those gentlemen the whole merit resulting from these negotiations and treaties. The advantage and prosperity of our employers, we declare to have been our sole object at heart. We are equally happy whoever be the agents in promoting them; and sincerely and cordially wish they may be established on the most permanent footing, and that the benefits derived to the Company may continue to the latest period.

The Select Committee having openly displayed their sense of authority over the Board, in taking before them the proceedings of Council, and canvassing the resolution relative to filling up the late vacancies, as we find, by an extract of their proceedings laid before the Council on the 16th September, they have been pleased to agree unanimously, " That the conduct of the members who composed the majority of the Board was highly improper and unbecoming, disrespectful to the Committee, and to the powers vested in them by the honourable Court of Directors." They further agreed, " That the behaviour of these gentlemen was dictated by a spirit of opposition to the Committee, since neither public nor private injury or benefit could arise from postponing the resolution; they are sorry to observe the slight effects produced by the lenity and moderation of their late proceedings,

"ceedings, and to see gentlemen in the
"highest stations in the service reduced
"to inconsistency in conduct and ar-
"gument for the sake of contradiction
"only. If implicit obedience was by
"those gentlemen thought due to the
"letter of the Company's instructions,
"how came they to neglect both the let-
"ter and spirit of the Company's express
"orders for signing the covenants, and
"at a juncture especially when obe-
"dience became necessary to the secu-
"rity of their own reputations?" The
Committee then proceed to assign their
reasons why the number of Council should
not be enlarged, for which we refer you
to their proceedings. And, lastly, as an
occasional majority was intentionally taken
advantage of in that resolution, they propose to the Board now to reconsider, whether the former resolutions should stand
good or be reversed?

Since the Committee claim the power
of considering the acts of the Board, and
of throwing so severe a censure on the
conduct of its majority, why did they
not, of themselves, reverse the resolution
in question, without referring it to the
Board?

Board? In this they acknowledge their want of authority: but as the power of cenſuring, and of repealing are lodged in the ſame body, they have either exceeded the limits of their commiſſion in the one, or have deviated from conſiſtency in their meaſure in the other, by an uncommon remiſſion of their privileges, in all other inſtances ſo ſtrictly ſupported.

In their cenſure they have aſcribed reaſons for our conduct which never had exiſtence, and which it is impoſſible they could ever be acquainted with; and for no other apparent cauſe, but becauſe the Board differed with them in opinion. If a majority meets with ſuch treatment for offering their ſentiments, when they do not happen to coincide with the voices of the Committee, what may every individual member of the Board expect, when he is ſo unfortunate as to entertain a different opinion from them? Or what freedom of thought can take place at a Board, where our ſtations afford us no protection from the ſevereſt reflections, cloathed with the utmoſt acrimony of expreſſion, and from the violence of ſentiments manifeſted by ſuch reflections?

We

We have in some preceding paragraph informed you of our true reasons for voting, that the vacancies should be filled up. In answer to the Committee, we shall further add, that it was impossible to acquiesce in the delay proposed without contradiction to our sentiments, in acknowledging, that the Committee had power to transfer the Company's concerns to the management of only such a number as they thought proper, or to make any alterations in the commission of government which, in order to give it the more validity, you were pleased to grant in such a formal manner.

The Committee observe, that no public or private injury, or benefit could arise from the postponement. There was then the less reason to invalidate the Company's commission, and infringe their orders, since no advantage would arise to the public from such a deviation, and there was the greater probability of our being impartial in what we were personally to reap no benefit from. But how far, in our opinion, it related to the public we have already mentioned; and the exclusion of the two next to Council
from

from their stations allotted by the Company, was also a privation of the honour and benefits you intended, which surely cannot but be deemed a private injury.

If the Committee, by the lenity and moderation of their late proceedings, mean, as it should seem, the tenderness with which they carried on their late enquiries concerning the presents, the only occasion they ever had to manifest how far they were actuated by lenity and moderation, we beg leave to refer to the honourable Company the degree of obligation the members of the former Board lie under to the gentlemen of the Committee, on that score, in the course of those enquiries, as well as in the general tenor of their behaviour.

The Committee quote our delay in signing the covenants, as an argument which ought to have induced us to delay our resolutions of compleating the number of the Board. We presume they consider the former as a breach of orders; and they surely could not imagine, that because we had erred once, that we should persist invariably in the error: rather ought we, convinced of our former mistake,

take, carefully to avoid falling into others in future. We may with equal justice apply their own way of reasoning to themselves. If they think the Company's orders admit of a deviation, how came they to condemn the former President and Council for the same opinion? or, if they thought deviation wrong, how came they now to support its propriety, and to censure the Board because they could not acquiesce in their sentiments on this occasion? Certain we are, the cases were very different. The instructions concerning the covenants were of very little concernment to the honourable Company: their nomination of a Council of the highest importance to the government of the settlement, to their prerogative, and to their constitution itself. We cannot help remarking here, the ungenerous advantage the Committee propose to themselves in reviewing what has been enquired into and determined; and what, therefore, ought not again to have been mentioned.

As to our reputations, hitherto they have stood the test, and we doubt not but they ever will. And notwithstanding their ungenteel reflection, we believe the

world

world will judge the late President and his Council were as capable of knowing what belonged to the security of their characters, and will find they will support them with as much integrity as the gentlemen of the Select Committee.

As reasons for keeping the number of Council reduced, the Committee advised the recallment of the Chiefs of Midnapore and Benaras, and, at Mr. Verelst's recommendation, proposed to withdraw the Chief and Council at Burdwan; alledging it unecessary, and a needless expence, to have a Member of Council residing there, since a junior servant can equally well conduct the business, under the inspection and orders of a supravisor. We do not think the two former very material: but deem the collection of a revenue, amounting to above four hundred thousand pounds sterling a year, a very fit object for the employment of a Member of the Board; and we think he ought constantly to reside there, that his mind being unengaged with any other business, he may be better qualified and more at leisure to attend to the collections, to the distribution of justice, and to the improvements

provements which so large a district must admit of. As to the expence of maintaining a Chief and Council there, if the allowances from the Rajah are deemed improper, suppose them placed upon the same footing with the other subordinates: the Company could never grudge a charge so trifling as would be incurred, beyond the pay and salary which the gentlemen who are from the Council must receive, wherever they be stationed: but argument is needless: Mr. Verelst is to be the sole supravisor, or in other words, chief, with a privilege unusual to the other subordinates, that of acting, at the same time, as a Member of the Board as well as of the Committee.

The increase of the recalled Members will keep up the number of Council at the Presidency to eight, as directed by the honourable Company: but as that number is the least ordered to remain on the spot, we think two others would have been very eligible, and not more than is necessary to discharge the different offices usually filled by Members of Council; besides, if ten reside in Calcutta, from the circumstances of ill health or other avocations,

tions, not more than eight will be found conftantly to attend the Board. This being confidered, the infringement of the commiffion of government appears fo mnch the more improper, as the alteration would be attended with no advantage.

The charge of our having made ufe of a cafual majority to fill up the vacancies, we totally difavow: every Member has a right to propofe what he thinks proper, and to give his opinion. When this motion was made, we could not, without facrificing our fentiments, give our confent to the propofal of the Committee, and our voices happened to coincide with the majority: but this allegation is equally applicable upon every divifion in Council; and we may with the fame propriety advance, that the gentlemen of the Select Committee now take the advantage of their majority at the Board to reverfe a former refolution.

Upon the whole, our fentiments have been fo oppofite to thofe of the Committee on the fubject of filling up the vacancies in Council, that if you approve of the one, you muft condemn the other.

Which

Which of us have thought and acted moſt conformably to your meaning and intent, or have ſupported their opinions with moſt juſtice, you muſt be judges. We ſhall only add, that the unmerited cenſures and reflections which the gentlemen of the Committee have loaded us with in their proceedings, and the ſevere terms in which they are expreſſed, as they do not leſſen the force of our arguments, ſo neither do they add weight to theirs; and with this remark we leave it to your determination.

To the many inſtances we have related of the proceedings of the Select Committee, we ſhall trouble you with but one more, at once expreſſive of their diſpoſition towards the Council, and confirming the motives we aſcribed to their conduct, as well as our idea of their intentions. Believing that all the differences which had hitherto ariſen betwixt the Council and the Committee took their riſe from the different conſtructions placed upon the Company's orders, Mr. Leyceſter gave in a minute to the Board, the 25th September, propoſing an expedient to put an end to all further altercations:

tions: he set forth, " That the honoura-
" ble Company having expresly directed,
" that the powers of the Select Committee
" should cease when peace and tranquilli-
" ty were restored, seemed evidently to re-
" strict their authority to the due manage-
" ment of whatever matters were condu-
" cive or relative to that important point;
" that therefore it did not appear their
" intention, that the Committee should
" exist after the war was brought to an
" end: and as, by the late peace with
" Shujah Dowlah, the views of the Com-
" pany in this appointment were accom-
" plished, he proposed, that the Com-
" mittee should be dissolved; however,
" if this did not prove agreeable to the
" Committee, he desired Lord Clive and
" the gentlemen who came with him
" from Europe, to explain to the Board
" their idea of the powers the Committee
" are invested with, the term intended for
" their duration, and the particular busi-
" ness that belonged to their department.
" That it should then be put to the vote,
" whether the Committee should continue
" on such a footing, or not. The Mem-
" bers of the Committee themselves, being

" the

"the majority of Council then present, could give what weight they pleased to such a representation, and that after such a resolution, which would give a sanction to his acquiescence, he should never again give the Board, or himself further trouble in such debates. And that he was anxious to have this decided before the dispatch of the Admiral Steevens, that our honourable Masters might see the expediency of being as explicit as possible in the orders they shall give in consequence of this dispute."

Mr. Leycester's proposal can in no shape whatever be construed into an attack on the powers granted by the honourable Company to the Committee. The Board, of whom the members of the Committee formed the majority, were only called upon to give their idea of their extent. Nothing surely could be more reasonable, or better calculated to put an end to all debates; but the Committee would not agree to either one or other of the alternatives. They absolutely refused to give us any satisfaction whatever, relative to the powers by which they acted. They told

told us, that they themselves, and not the Board, were the judges when the powers of the Committee ought to cease; and that they would answer to the Court of Directors, not to us, on the subject of Mr. Leycester's minute.

We cannot, without sincere concern, reflect on the situation we are reduced to. We have before us your instructions, the sense of which seems very obvious to us; and it is our duty to enforce and support these, as far as our abilities can reach. We see the Select Committee pursuing measures which appear to us contrary to those instructions; and when we represent our opinion, and request an explanation, the Committee persist in denying us any access to information.

We have frequently received from those gentlemen verbal accounts of the powers they tell us the Company determined they should be invested with. Why do they decline to authenticate these on the face of the consultations, when thus called upon? since it would put an end to our debates. Do they not give us room to imagine, that they do not chuse publicly to avow an extent of power so far beyond the

the limit of your orders, by an explanation which cannot be supported by the tenor of your instructions? In this disagreeable dilemma, what path is left for us to tread? If, in strict conformity to our sentiments, we assert the authority of the Company's orders, we are accused of acting from the spirit of opposition and contradiction. If we acquiesce in the proceedings of the Committee, we trespass against our own conviction, and our sense of the duty we owe to our employers. Which shall we prefer, the faithful discharge of the trust reposed in us, whilst subjected to injury, or the purchase of our peace and quiet, at the expence of our opinions and characters? Would the world, or could we ourselves applaud such insincerity?

We cannot regard the instances we have given you of the Committee's exercise of the power set forth, but as highly improper, whether we consider the immediate effects or example they yield. A set of gentlemen, whom you appointed to carry on the war you understood this settlement to be engaged in, and to effect a peace, when that war could be brought

brought to a conclusion, instead of restricting themselves to the points committed to their care, assume the power to regulate every branch of your concerns, independently of your Council. Setting aside entirely the term you prescribe to their authority, they allow themselves only to be the judges when it should end. The whole power is in their hands, and they may employ it to what purposes, and as long as they please, nor can your Council restrain them. We mean not to say, that the gentlemen who now compose the Select Committee will use their power for any bad design, but we think they afford a dangerous precedent, by the success of an authority not founded on your orders, which may, one time or other, prove very detrimental to your affairs.

We cannot avoid complaining of our situation, prevented as we are from doing our duty, in the management of affairs you were pleased to commit to our charge; exposed to censures and reflections for difference in opinion; the former administration condemned and disparaged, in order to raise the credit of the present. A groundless alarm, therefore,

fore, is raised, of the extreme danger the settlement is threatened with, from impending ruin. No other refutation to this assertion is required, than to look back on the success with which we maintained a war against one of the most formidable Princes in Hindostan; a stronger test of the firmness of our government than was ever before experienced: and we made provision for one of the most ample investments the honourable Company have received from Bengal for a considerable time.

And, as if by way of comparison, his Lordship sets forth in strong colours, the great disinterestedness of the gentlemen associated with him in the Select Committee. We do not want to derogate from the merits of those gentlemen; but in order to obviate the oblique reflection cast upon the former President and his Council by his Lordship's declaration, we must remark, that Mr. Verelst is appointed to the Chiefship of Burdwan and to the office of export warehouse-keeper, two of the most advantageous employs in your service, and which were always before held separate; and we understand that the Chiefship of Coffimbuzar, and residence at the Durbar are to be united in the person of Mr. Sykes.

Although to the behaviour of the Committee, as we have related, we could not, confiftently either with our duty to you or to the juftice we owe our own characters, acquiefce or fubmit; yet we have invariably made it a maxim to conduct ourfelves with the greateft moderation whenever, to our concern, we were under a necessity of expressing our diffent from their proceedings; and where we have difapproved of their political meafures, we have induftrioufly avoided a public diffent at the Board, in order to prevent the ill confequences which have oft heretofore arifen from the difcovery of a contrariety, or difference of fentiments in the Council on thefe fubjects; whence room has frequently been given to difcontented people to look for alterations from every change in our government, and to our enemies, to make their utmoft advantage of fuch contending parties. And referving for our own honour and vindication this declaration now made to you, we would neither wifh, nor attempt

tempt any innovation in the plan fixed on by the Committee, for the same reasons as we objected to the infringement of former engagements, considering almost every change as attended with bad consequences.

We beg you will not consider this remonstrance as flowing from a desire to keep up the divisions which have subsisted among us, or from any spirit of resentment, or recrimination. We most heartily despise such mean motives, and shall never permit them to influence our conduct. Our only view herein is to give you particular information concerning the debates which have arisen on the intent and meaning of your orders, and that you may see the necessity of being as full and explicit as possible in your instructions on this, and on similar occasions: and we desire you will be perfectly assured, that though the Committee, instead of endeavouring to conciliate their subversion of our measures, have given us much unnecessary disgust, yet having thus referred ourselves to you, we shall, on our part, bury in oblivion all that is past, shall be ready to concur with heart

and

and hand to make the Committee's regulations anſwer the moſt ſalutary ends, and to ſtudy at the revival of that harmony and good underſtanding ſo eſſential for the reputation of our government, and the ſucceſs of your affairs.

And now, honourable Sirs, having given you a ſtatement of matters, conformably to the ſtricteſt truth, we think it neceſſary to inform you, we are no leſs concerned to be under the neceſſity of making our application to you in this unuſal manner, than for the occaſion which has obliged us to take ſuch an uncuſtomary ſtep. But we reſolved, as already mentioned, to avoid as much as poſſible the appearance of diſputes and diſſenſions at the Council Board, and ſenſible that the many altercations with which the proceedings of Council have heretofore been filled, muſt prove as diſagreeable to you as they are to the parties concerned, we determined not to waſte that time and attention in fruitleſs debates at the Board, which ought to be devoted to the management of your buſineſs; and we deem it the moſt eligible, as the more moderate, to to reſerve for the firſt conveyance to

Europe

Europe our intention of communicating to you the subject of our disagreements; and, conscious that all our measures have been regulated by a sincere and warm attachment to your advantages and interests, we most cheerfully refer our proceedings to the decision of your candour and justice, and appeal to you, whether we have acted with propriety, or not? At the same time, we dare to assure you, that whatever advantages or superiority of interest, power, or station may afford others over us, in rendering you services, there are none whose hearts are filled with a more fervent zeal for your prosperity than ourselves.

We have the honour to be, with the utmost respect,

Honourable Sirs,

Your most faithful,

most devoted,

and most obedient,

humble servants,

(Signed,) { RALPH LEYCESTER, GEORGE GRAY.

Calcutta, the 29th September, 1765.

POSTSCRIPT.

THE above addrefs was wrote before the difpatch of the Admiral Stevens, and intended to have been forwarded to you by that fhip; but refolving to proceed with the utmoft caution, left fome circumftances overlooked by us, or a poffible miftake in regard to your orders, might give Lord Clive a pretext to gratify a refentment againft us which we had reafon to think already formed, we delayed tranfmitting our addrefs by that conveyance: and as either a confirmation or reverfion of your orders might fo foon be expected, in anfwer to the interefting advices conveyed you by the fhips of the feafon, 1763-4, we determined to wait for an intelligence which could not fail to inform us of your intentions, beyond the poffibility of a doubt.

Your commands accordingly, of the 15th February, *per* Grenville, fully confirmed

firmed us in our sentiments, that Lord Clive had assumed an authority which was by no means your intention, and deprived your Council of that share of the administration which you had allotted them, by transferring the reins of government into the hands of a Select Committee. Had you ever intended or seen it necessary, that this body should have continued the extensive authority which they now exercise, we think it will not bear a doubt, but that you would have addressed them separately, and invested them with full powers at a juncture so critical as the mutiny of our army and the invasion of Shujah Dowlah, the advice of which events then lay before you, and conveyed an alarming prospect. Whereas your commands are directed, as usual, to the whole Council, whom you order to see them executed: and, in the 47th paragraph, you express your approbation of the method of conducting your affairs by the channels of a public and private department, under the direction of the President and Council. Had you meant to invest the Committee with the authority they have assumed, this would not, we conceive, have been the mode of your orders. They would certainly have been delegated in that ample and accurate form which was obferved with refpect to Mr. Vanfittart, in the year 1763: and from their not being fo, we are the more confirmed in the belief, that you will approve of our fentiments regarding the proceedings of Lord Clive, and the powers exercifed by the Select Committee.

The peace with Shujah Dowlah was certainly the proper and natural period to the authority of the Select Committee, had it been exercifed within the bounds prefcribed by your appointment. But Lord Clive, fetting afide thefe orders, has thought proper to continue it; for what reafon we cannot conceive, unlefs upon the principle, that his own power becomes the greater from it than if the adminiftration was in the hands of the whole Council.

From the fame reafon it would appear, that thofe branches of the Company's bufinefs which ought not only to be made known, but in which your fervants ought actually to be inftructed, are become matters of the utmoft fecrecy. Inftead of collecting

lecting the sentiments of the Council on a branch so highly important as the revenues are now rendered, and which, in conformity to your express commands, has heretofore been managed by a Committee of the Board, the Members of the Council are kept in ignorance of the manner in which the provinces are settled, or the income the Company ought to receive from them, so far at least as the Committee are able to conceal from them any knowledge in these affairs. We cannot here avoid remarking, that though in September the Board were unanimously of opinion, that the presence of a Member of the Board was unnecessary at Midnapore, yet the Committee have since taken the matter under their consideration, and sent Mr. Verelst to supervise the settlement of the collections, though they were committed to Mr. Graham, a gentleman of approved integrity and abilities, as will appear as well from your own sentiments as from the opinion of the Board, on Mr. Graham's conduct while he had charge of Burdwan, and acted in the employ of secretary to the Council. It appears to us highly improper thus to conceal from the Members of the

Board the system of the collections which must one day come under their inspection, as the Company are thereby deprived of any benefit they might reap from the knowledge of their other servants; and they (the servants) are denied an opportunity of that experience, or improvement which they might acquire, and which must, sooner or later, be dedicated to the Company's service.

You will observe by the foregoing letter, which was wrote before the Admiral Stevens sailed, our fixed determination to avoid all manner of disputes, and to aim at the revival of that harmony so much to be wished amongst those who have the administration of your affairs abroad. It was on the point of the Admiral Stevens dispatch, that Lord Clive gave us reason to doubt the efficacy of our best intentions. He appeared determined to protrude all possibility of a reconciliation: and incensed with the freedom and independence of sentiment we had dared to assert, in opposition to his opinion, it seemed, to all appearance, that he was resolved either to disgust into resignation, or to drive from the service those who were acting upon

upon principles and maxims different from his own. We forefaw the fame fyftem of violence which had been exercifed in regard to Mooteram, Mr. Johnftone's fervant, was about to be ufed upon Ramanaut, Mr. Gray's, who was feized with military guards on the September, and is ftill detained a prifoner, expófed to a power which every member of a free community muft abhor.

The various minutes which have paffed between Lord Clive and Mr. Gray on this fubject, ftand entered on the face of the confultations, and we beg leave to refer you to thefe for particular information. We fhall only trouble you here with fome few remarks, in order to fet the difpute in a clear and impartial point of view. That Lord Clive was feverely exafperated againft the gentlemen of the Board, who had difagreed with him in feveral points, may, we think, be feen in the tenor of a minute of his fent to the Board during his ftay at Illihabad, and entered in confultation of 22d July, as well as in the extract of the proceedings of the Select Committee, laid before the Board the 16th September. He had, in fearch we

fuppofe

suppose for charges against the members of the prior administration, given ear to complaints against Mr. Gray, which were given out to be of a most extraordinary nature, and propagated in such manner as if he hoped they might serve as a check upon that gentleman's opinion. He doubtless took for granted, or wished to believe, that what he heard was true; for he insinuated them to others, perhaps with a view that Mr. Gray himself should hear, that such complaints had been made; but without ever giving Mr. Gray the least hint, or information on the subject. At last, Mr. Gray, determining to remain no longer under such injurious imputations, thought it highly necessary that he should call upon Lord Clive to produce his complaints before the Board. His Lordship pretended, that he was in actual possession of charges against Mr. Gray at that time; but instead of producing such at the next Council, the first step he took was to confine Ramanaut, one of Mr. Gray's servants, under a military guard: where, as his servants set forth to Mr. Gray, he was insulted, terrified with the idea of the severest punishments,

ments, forced to give money to the guards over him, denied all accefs but from people belonging to Lord Clive, who taking advantage of his unfortunate situation, again and again fuggefted to him, that if he would prefent informations to his lordfhip he would be releafed and eafed of his troubles. At the fame time we heard meafures were taken, at Moorfhadabad and in different parts of the country, to obtain complaints from many who had had connections with Mr. Gray, as indeed appears by letters that gentleman received from fome of thofe people, who had an opportunity of writing to him. This tenor of conduct can never fail to appear to the world in its real light, when it is remarked, that his Lordfhip (deviating from the requeft made by Mr. Gray, that he would inform the Board of the complaints he actually had heard) appeared to feek refource in a fyftem the moft injurious; to encourage frefh complaints, to declare at the Board his determination in the courfe of their fcrutiny to lay *his humanity* afide, and in conformity to fo extraordinary a fentiment, to invite men, as we apprehend, to give information

information which they themselves seem never to have thought of; glossing over the procedure with the specious pretence, that he is ready and willing to hearken to and redress all complaints that are laid before him. We need only mention the instance of Bulakidass, to illustrate what we here remark. This man had received a Perwanah from Lord Clive himself to reside at Calcutta, yet did his Lordship, when he returned from Illihabad, for purposes unknown to us, privately send a messenger to turn Bulakidass out of the settlement, when he apprehended his life to be in the most imminent danger by such expulsion. Mr. Gray, from the motives set forth in his minute of the 4th November, gave him shelter in one of the Pergumahs near Calcutta; but in his retreat being discovered, after Mr. Gray's call on Lord Clive, he was sent for by his Lordship, and admitted to an audience: with what view we cannot devise, unless to procure from him matter of information against Mr. Gray. Bulakidass was accordingly soon after produced as Mr. Gray's accuser, on certain transactions: but when he came before the Board, it

must

must appear, from the testimony he made on oath, notwithstanding Lord Clive's favour might be in competition, that he considered Mr. Gray as the saver of his life and honour: and can it be imagined, that under the sense of such an obligation, recently received, Bulakidass would voluntarily have offered a complaint against Mr. Gray? As to Ramanaut, he was charged with malpractices; and, without a hearing, punished with a military imprisonment for above two months; then brought with guards before the Council, and under these circumstances allowed to declare himself guilty of perjury, in an oath he had taken before a justice of the peace in matters relative to Mr. Gray: and though he was the person accused, yet, setting aside charges against him, he is brought as an evidence against Mr. Gray, and his menial servants and relations are produced to corroborate his information.

Mr. Gray, on the 4th October, proposed sundry questions to the Board, touching the governor's prerogative and right of using military guards over men not subject to martial law? Instead of a candid

candid difquifition, and unbiaffed fentiments on a point of fuch infinite importance to our civil liberty, General Carnac and Mr. Verelft were of opinion, that the queftions themfelves were highly unbecoming, and infolent to the Prefident; and, upon a reference to the Board, as a bench of the King's juftices, on the 18th October, it was the opinion of the majority, that the depofitions then made with regard to Mr. Gray's fervant, whofe houfe was befet with a body of men in arms, and whofe property had been taken away, that depofitions of fuch a nature (made by two gentlemen who had been eye-witneffes of this breach of the peace) were not fufficient grounds on which to found a warrant. It really gives us pain to refer to the proceedings of a bench of juftices, whofe determination muft feem to authorize the ufe of military guards in a manner that we all along, hitherto, confidered as the higheft infult upon a free government. Mr. Gray had placed fuch firm belief in obtaining redrefs from the King's juftices, that it was extreme mortification to him to find the inquiry he had to complain of, in a manner, fanctified

fied by the opinion of those gentlemen on whom he placed his chief dependence, from considering them as guardians of the peace, and protectors of our laws.

In the course of the debates on the questions proposed by Mr. Gray, on the 14th, Lord Clive and General Carnac asserted this to be a military as well as civil government. Such declarations, in defence of a conduct so unprecedented and oppressive, from the two military Members of the Board, who, from the authority assumed by the Select Committee, were become arbiters of the settlement, raised the liveliest apprehension, that these gentlemen were adopting maxims in justification of the use of military guards over civil subjects that were totally incompatible with our laws, and inconsistent with our charter of justice. Mr. Leycester, having been more particularly injured by some extraordinary declarations of General Carnac, thought it incumbent on him, in the following Council, to remind the Board of what had passed, and to call on Lord Clive and General Carnac for an explanation of the assertions they had made the preceding day, touching military authority. The immediate

immediate difavowal of any ill intent in such affertions was what Mr. Leycefter might reasonably have expected from Lord Clive. In this however he was difappointed: and his Lordfhip's filence on a point of fuch infinite importance naturally confirmed the apprehenfion already entertained of his intentions. Let his Lordfhip's filence proceed from whatever caufe, he treated Mr. Leycefter's minute with great indifference; and, provoked with feeing his declaration fo warmly oppofed by that gentleman, he feemed refolved to terminate the debate in a manner that fhould moft injure the gentleman who had expofed his Lordfhip's indifcretion, in betraying his fentiments on fuch a fubject. After allowing Mr. Leycefter's minute to lay unnoticed for ten days, fo that the fubject of the debate became fully known in town, and exaggerated with all the embellifhments which frequent repetition, and mens natural anxieties on a point of fuch general concernment were fure to raife, Lord Clive, General Carnac and Mr. Verelft feem to have come agreed in a determination to fufpend Mr. Leycefter the fervice, as evidently appeared from

the

the course of that day's proceedings. They brought their several minutes ready prepared, and numbered as they were to be entered. The sentence of suspension was wrote before the Council met; and, in a most unprecedented manner, a paragraph was also brought ready wrote for a general letter, to be sent two or three months afterwards, with their sentiments and detail for your information, anticipating in their private resolutions the determination of the Board. Stronger proofs cannot be given of his Lordship's intent to take advantage of his occasional majority; though it is a measure he himself heretofore condemned in others, as may be collected from the severe, though unjust censure he threw upon the gentlemen who voted for compleating the number of the Members of Council. We beg leave to refer to the proceedings of the 28th October, 4th November, and to Mr. Leycester's letter, in consequence of his suspension, for a full explanation of all this proceeding, entered in consultation of the 5th December; and shall only further add, that Mr. Leycester was condemned unheard; that a minute he several times

offered

offered to be read in courſe of debate, was rejected by the Preſident, till the minutes of himſelf and friends were read, and the ſentiments of the Board collected, and that the gentlemen who had been accuſed, ſet in judgment on their accuſer, and formed the majority who ſuſpended him.

To a meaſure ſo arbitrary and unjuſt, thoſe members of the Board who were unbiaſſed by party ſhowed their diſapprobation by their diſſents. Mr. Gray, now the only remaining member of thoſe whom Lord Clive ſeemed to conſider as obnoxious to him, conceived, from the treament Mr. Leyceſter had met with, that he might ſoon expect the ſame fate, from the plan of the party formed in ſupport of Lord Clive. He ſaw, with concern, that Board, which ought to deliberate on the meaſures proper for your intereſts, gratifying their own reſentments, throwing obloquy on men who had ſerved you with honour and fidelity, in order to enhance their own merits and qualifications; though perhaps it may appear to you, they promote their own power, rather than conſult the Company's advantage.

He

He saw himself and the independent members of the Board deprived of that share in the management of your affairs which, from the tenor of your orders, he considered as his right; and which seem now, as if intended only to be conferred on those who pay a most implicit submission to the sentiments and dictates of the President. Heartily disgusted, therefore, with the maxims adopted, he preferred a resignation to an abject compliance with measures his heart could not approve of. He accordingly took his leave of the Board in a minute, delivered in the 4th November, to which we beg leave particularly to refer you. However, that no ill construction should be put on Mr. Gray's abdication at that time, he desired the enquiries into his conduct, begun by Lord Clive, should be continued. What has been since done in these enquiries Mr. Gray has but a day or two been informed of, and therefore has not yet been able to make any reply.

The independent members of the Board being out of the service, Lord Clive seems now to have an established majority linked to him by the strongest ties. General Carnac

Carnac is avowedly attached to Lord Clive, as muſt appear in the ſtrongeſt as well as moſt extraordinary light, when that ſudden and extreme change in his opinion of things, produced immediately on his Lordſhip's arrival, be conſidered. We need only deſire you will compare General Carnac's minutes during the time of Mr. Vanſittart's government, and his ſentiments before Lord Clive's arrival, with his preſent acquieſcence in his Lordſhip's meaſures; particularly thoſe relative to the country government, to convince you of the truth of this.

General Carnac, on a former occaſion, was of opinion, that to give the officers of the Nabob's government an authority over European agents, and even over Black Gomaſtahs, was diſhonourable to our nation, and ſubmitting to an oppreſſion. Mr. Verelſt was, but a few months ago, of opinion, that European agents were far more eligible than Black Gomaſtahs, and that they ought by no means to be recalled. Yet now we find both theſe gentlemen concurring in opinion, that European agents are a ſource of oppreſſion, and an occaſion of alarm to the natives;

natives; and have refolved, that thofe Europeans who go up on the fervice of the Society of Trade, and of courfe will at all times be under the orders of the members of the Board, fhall in every difpute appeal to the arbitrary decifion of the officers of the country government. It may be alledged, that the change of the fyftem of government may occafion an alteration of circumftances: but we do not allow any fuch change has taken place as to alter the manners and difpofitions of the people, who can be no further fenfible of change than, that Mahomed Reza Cawn is the head, inftead of Najum o' Dowlah. When the members of our own government exprefs fentiments of fuch contempt for their own countrymen, we cannot expect, that the natives will entertain any regard or refpect for them: but, on the contrary, catching the idea from fuch declarations, will confider them as caufes of debate, and objects of their hatred; and will take every opportunity to injure and infult them.

The ample provifion made for Mr. Verelft and Mr. Sykes, evinces how much Lord Clive has it in his power to indulge those who, coinciding with him in sentiment, are so happy as to gain his Lordship's approbation and favour. He seems, therefore, to have established a power that, as we conceive, gives him too great a sway, not only over measures, but the declaration of opinions; for to many it will appear inconvenient, if not dangerous to deliver sentiments different from his Lordship's, as they may apprehend it a means of incurring his displeasure, at the expence of their future prospects. A system that may reduce your servants to a state of dependence on your Governors, tends only to render your Councils useless and unnecessary; unless to give a sanction to measures, by implicitly approving whatever they are pleased to propose.

Whether the object of Lord Clive's reformation is the reducing your Council to a state of dependence on himself, and assuming into his own hands all their powers, will appear to you from the tenor of his conduct. He has promoted and indulged those who have supported him in the authority he has assumed; and we have already pointed out to you how

he

he has demeaned himself towards those who have differed from him in opinion. Of his resentments we have given you some instances. We shall only mention one example of his partiality to friends, in the instance of General Carnac; when during the course of enquiries into Mr. Gray's conduct, General Carnac asked Mr. Gray, if he knew of the covenants when he accepted the present from the Nabob? implying thereby, that if he did know, he ought not to have received it. Mr. Gray, in return, demanded of the General, if he had received a present from Bulwantsing, whether he did not know of the covenants then; and if it was not at a time when he was actually settling with that Rajah for the revenues of his country? Had his Lordship been actuated by a real impartiality, and desire of reforming abuses, such an imputation would never have been suffered to remain unnoticed: but it was not for his Lordship's purpose to point out the want of disinterestedness in his friends, which he appears desirous to discover in his opposers. When General Carnac left Calcutta to command the army, in January 1765, his first letter to the

the Board was to express his disapprobation of any treaty with Bulwantsing, considering him as a man on whose attachment we could have no reliance. Previous to this, the Board had declared their dislike also to any connection with Bulwantsing; and that, if the commanding officer had not already entered into a treaty with him, it was their desire that he should not. Notwithstanding this conformity of sentiment, one of the first steps the General took, after he reached the army, was to enter into fresh articles with Bulwantsing, which were ratified before the Board gave their concurrence: and does not the General leave room to suppose, from his silence touching Mr. Gray's questions, that it was on this occasion he either received or was promised the present from Bulwantsing, amounting to a very large sum? We must here mention that the covenants were drawn out for all your servants on this establishment, civil as well as military, dated the 9th May. Those for the officers were sent up to the army: and though General Carnac called on his officers to execute theirs, yet we believe he has not to this

this day signed them himself; at least he did not execute them at the same time, nor had he signed them a few days ago. So glaring a partiality requires a very particular explanation, especially when his Lordship has carried his desire of seeing the covenants put into execution over others to such a length, as to bind up the hands of even the surgeons in the service from receiving presents from the dependants of the government, whose profession excludes them from any share of administration, and whose advantages arise chiefly from presents, in consideration of their care and attendance.

We must here take notice of a source of power and influence which any governor, in the present state of affairs, has over your other servants, that of stopping the trade in the country of any who become obnoxious to him. His authority over the officers of the government will lead them eagerly to anticipate his resentments, and a hint to them will suffice. The correspondence with the officers being confined to the governor, he has it in his option to give what private orders he pleases, and which would be certainly obeyed,

obeyed, without his name ever appearing. Such is his power over the inhabitants of this country: and such the nature of the people, that every one will be ready to bear testimony to whatever they think will be agreeable to him. Thus he bears the most absolute command over the trade and fortunes of your servants without controul, which appears to us a very dangerous sway.

Hitherto, notwithstanding the vacancies which have lately happened in council, no measures are taken to fill them up; whilst the number of Members of the Board in Calcutta is too small to fill the different offices heretofore allotted them, or to complete the Select Committee's own plan of reduction. We can ascribe no reason for this, unless it is intended to pursue the same system in the appointment of the Members of the Board, which has been done in other branches. The succession to Council may probably be rendered dependent on Lord Clive: the nomination to which, with all posts of advantage, he will naturally bestow as a matter of favour and interest: and as more compliance may be expected from those gentlemen

tlemen called to the Board out of their rank, who muſt neceſſarily conſider themſelves obliged to Lord Clive for their promotion, than from thoſe who will conſider their ſucceeding to the vacant ſeats as matter of right, ſo we apprehend that the gentlemen who, by your appointment, ſtand firſt in the liſt of ſucceſſion, run the greateſt riſque of being injured and deprived of their right. The juſtice of this remark muſt depend on the event: but it is not, we think, unnatural to ſuppoſe Lord Clive will commit this deviation from your orders, when, in our ſenſe of them, he has ſo far exceeded their bounds already, that it would ſeem as if he thought himſelf far ſuperior to them, and indifferent to the opinion you entertain of his conduct.

We are unwilling to treſpaſs longer on your patience, by enumerating further inſtances of the power exerciſed in the preſent ſyſtem of government, as we believe what we have mentioned will be ſufficient to give you a true idea of the occaſion of our differences in opinion from Lord Clive. The diſregard paid to your orders, and ſubverſion of the regulations

by

by which your settlement has heretofore been governed, affords, we think, a precedent that may prove fatal to your affairs. We hope very soon for an opportunity to represent what further occurs upon this subject in person, being forced, by the conduct of your President, from this settlement; where we have suffered many hardships in your service, and have made it our study to promote the welfare and interest of our masters to the utmost of our power and ability. The injuries and wrongs we have ourselves received, we submit entirely to your candour and justice: but we cannot conclude without expressing our uneasiness for the state of your settlement and situation of your servants, subjected to the will and pleasure of gentlemen who thus deviate from your established rules, and employ the power you have put into their hands in a manner, as we apprehend, so contrary to your intentions.

The above was all wrote, and we were on the point of closing this address, when letters came in from Madrass, advising of a circumstance that has thrown the settlement into a flame: it appears, that the

Select

Select Committee have invited to take rank in your service at Bengal, four of the Madrass servants, who are now on their way hither. This measure is so glaring a proof of the truth of our foregoing remarks, and apprehensions of the power assumed by Lord Clive and the Committee, that we cannot help pointing it out to you. We consider this as the most dangerous step that could possibly have been taken; for we cannot find, either from your commission of government or from a reference to your former orders, that you ever conferred on your Presidents and Councils a power of appointing civil servants, far less of calling gentlemen from another establishment to fill up vacated seats at the Board. Without depreciating the merits of the gentlemen now invited, on their own establishment, we may venture to assert, that their inexperience in your concerns here must render them less qualified to serve you in such high stations, than your servants who have been long engaged in promoting your interests in Bengal; and in age and standing in your service, some of the gentlemen who are now called down from Madrass

D d
are

are not superior on their own establishment to those now superseded in this. And upon a comparison of the list of your Madrass servants with those on this establishment, it appears, that the oldest writer in Bengal is the 27th from Council, the oldest writer at Madrass is also the 27th, including the four gentlemen now called down: and of seven years standing there are twenty in Bengal and twenty-one at Madrass.

When merit is alledged as the reason for promotion, it affords a pretext for partiality in the choice, more especially when the power of promoting rests in the hands of a few, whose proceedings are kept secret, and who will not publickly declare their reasons. The abuse of authority in so unheard-of, and illegal an appointment, the insult and indignity done to a whole settlement, the spirit of dissension it must foment, and the discouragement it must give to that zeal in you servants which is the surest source of your success, are all circumstances too obvious to escape your consideration. We may venture to pronounce, that the measure is by no means calculated for your advantage, though it may

may promise to secure Lord Clive a majority in Council that will approve of, and coincide in all his measures; since these gentlemen will probably consider themselves bound in gratitude to support that power which raised them, as his lordship must the resolution he has had the principal share in effecting. We leave it to you to determine, whether it is probable Lord Clive himself can deem this a step calculated for the interests of the Company, after the declaration of his sentiments made to you in his address of the 27th April, 1764. He there declares it his opinion, that the supercession of your Bengal servants from another settlement was the source of the unfortunate parties and discontents that had prevailed in Calcutta; that the appointment of Mr. Spencer from Bombay could not fail to increase those evils, and that the Company's affairs could only prosper from unanimity and harmony amongst the servants abroad. Is it possible but that he must conceive the same cause will still produce the same effects? that he can consider a measure right in him which he thought wrong in his masters? or that he can even expect an acquiefcence to his will and pleafure in this point, which he feemed to think you, our mafters, had no reafon to look for?

The civil fervants in all your prefidencies have heretofore confidered you as the fole arbiters of rank and ftanding; they have hitherto deemed themfelves indebted to your favour for the ftations which you were pleafed to allot them; and they have, till now, been fupported by you in a regular gradation, except in extraordinary cafes, where, on perfect conviction, you might be forced to deviate from the rules you yourfelves had laid down. Does not Lord Clive appear, in this inftance, to affume to himfelf this power and prerogative, and to be turning the fource of dependence from you to himfelf? If your fervants lay thus at his devotion, be you the judges whofe intereft and views they will moft readily promote. The body of fervants fenfibly feeling this unmerited injury and difgrace, look forward, with firm affurance of obtaining redrefs from you: and your countenance to, or difapprobation of this meafure measure must determine whom they are to consider as their masters.

The servants having on this subject drawn up an appeal to you, Lord Clive has taken care to express his displeasure at this measure, by intimating to several, it would have been better if they had not subscribed to it. If he considers it as a measure right in itself, or as one that you would approve, we do not think he would have used any means to discourage his fellow-servants from complaining, of what they think an injury, to their common masters. The servants, on all occasions, should place the firmest reliance on your candor and justice; and to presume to discountenance an intercourse you have ever admitted, is such an attempt to conceal from you the ideas men have of this proceeding, as cannot possibly escape your notice.

Sensible of the many favours and benefits we have received in your service, we beg leave once more to express our most grateful acknowledgments. We shall be very solicitous to find, that our services have met with your approbation, and

shall

shall ever entertain the most fervent wishes for the welfare and prosperity of the Company's affairs.

We have the honour to be, with the utmost respect,

Honourable Sirs,

Your most faithful,

most devoted,

and most obedient,

humble servants,

(Signed,) { RALPH LEYCESTER,
George Gray.

Fort William, 14th January 1766.

www.ingramcontent.com/pod-product-compliance
Lightning Source LLC
Chambersburg PA
CBHW031812230426
43669CB00009B/1111